# Monopolistic Competition and Macroeconomic Theory

Much of today's conventional macroeconomic theory presumes that markets for goods approach the state of perfect competition. *Monopolistic Competition and Macroeconomic Theory* assumes that markets are imperfect, so that sellers have some power over price, and must therefore form quantity expectations about the location of the firm's demand curve.

The question is then about the macroeconomic implications of imperfect competition in goods markets. The first chapter is a brief survey of ideas recently proposed in economics including multiple equilibria. The second chapter describes a particular micro-based macro model that allows several families of equilibria. The third chapter shows how a standard locational model can be used to describe a sample macroeconomy when firms have close rivals.

In this volume derived from his Federico Caffé Lectures, Nobel Laureate Robert Solow shows that there are simple and tractable micro-based models that offer the possibility of a richer and more intuitive macroeconomics.

**Robert M. Solow** is Institute Professor Emeritus, Massachusetts Institute of Technology Department of Economics. He is a former President of the American Economic Association, and Econometric Society and the current President of the International Economic Association. In 1987 he was awarded the Alfred Nobel Memorial Prize in Economic Science.

D1114376

## Federico Caffè Lectures

This series of annual lectures was initiated to honour the memory of Federico Caffè. They are jointly sponsored by the Department of Public Economics at the University of Rome, where Caffè held a chair from 1959 to 1987, and the Bank of Italy, where he served for many years as an adviser. The publication of the lectures will provide a vehicle for leading scholars in the economics profession, and for the interested general reader, to reflect on the pressing economic and social issues of the times.

# Monopolistic Competition and Macroeconomic Theory

Robert M. Solow

**CAMBRIDGE**
UNIVERSITY PRESS

PUBLISHED BY THE PRESS SYNDICATE OF THE UNIVERSITY OF CAMBRIDGE
The Pitt Building, Trumpington Street, Cambridge, United Kingdom

CAMBRIDGE UNIVERSITY PRESS
The Edinburgh Building, Cambridge CB2 2RU, UK    http://www.cup.cam.ac.uk
40 West 20th Street, New York, NY 10011–4211, USA    http://www.cup.org
10 Stamford Road, Oakleigh, Melbourne 3166, Australia

First published 1998
Reprinted 1999

Printed in the United Kingdom at the University Press, Cambridge

Typeset in Melior 10/13pt    [CE]

A catalogue record for this book is available from the British Library

ISBN 0 521 62338 3 hardback
ISBN 0 521 62616 1 paperback

# Contents

# Introduction

How can one explain the fact that Keynesian ideas and methods have survived for sixty years despite their theoretical weaknesses and analytical crudities? These defects have been pointed out again and again, beginning with the first reviews of the *General Theory* and continuing to the present day. Still, most of the viable macro models used for forecasting and policy analysis are recognizably Keynesian in structure, if not in every detail. The various multipliers would not be strange to someone whose intuition had grown up in some version of ISLM, though some numerical values might be unexpected. In the meanwhile, *avant-garde* academic macroeconomic theory is long gone, mostly pursuing alternatives – new-Classical macroeconomics, real business-cycle theory – that have crudities and weaknesses of their own, but that cling to the ideas of standard competitive theory. So why does the older way of thinking persist?

One reason is, no doubt, the repeated commonsense perception that things are just not the way that standard competitive theory claims that they are. The contrast is especially strong in recessions, but it is present more of the time than that. I choose just one commonplace example, because it suits my purpose, not for any deeper reason. In any recession, it is all too obvious that most business firms would be happy to produce and sell more than they are currently able to sell at the current price. Evidently, then, price exceeds marginal cost. Why do firms not quote lower prices to

1

increase sales? Perhaps if all of them did so, the aggregate results would be all-around deflation and nothing else. (The Pigou effect or the Keynes effect might come into play, but that is a different story, not about individual firms.) Still, one is entitled to ask: Why does price reduction not happen?

If you asked the firm directly – assuming firms could talk – it might give one of several answers. It believes it faces a very inelastic demand curve; firms often say that. It might even be true for some firms; but then it is clear that competition cannot be the right market form for describing the sort of situation that we call a recession.

Or else the firm could say that any price cut on its part would merely elicit matching price reductions from its rivals, or even something more aggressive, so it is better to leave things as they are. Once again, it may all be true; but then it is a mistake to use ideas drawn from competitive theory to analyze what does happen in a recession.

The firm might say something quite different: yes, it could improve sales and profits in the short run by price reduction, but it suspects that it would lose in the longer run because its customers would be annoyed at later price increases, and committed customers are very important in the long run. Or it might report that it needs an excess of price over marginal cost to cover the costs of maintaining some capacity that is sometimes idle because of the vagaries of consumer search. If any of these stories is true – and who are we to claim otherwise? – standard competitive theory will not help us to understand recessions.

On the other hand, the firm might say: "Why didn't I think of that?" and proceed to reduce prices.

These are not exactly deep thoughts. I mention them only to make two points that together amount almost to a small paradox.

(1) Keynesian ideas survive because the usual alternatives ask us to believe things that appear not to be true. ("Mis-

perceptions" stories seem to have disappeared for that reason.) The basic Keynesian building blocks, on the other hand, while no doubt lacking in theoretical refinement, seem rather closer to everyday observation. At least economists still estimate consumption functions, demand-for-money equations, and slow price-adjustment relations that are refinements, more or less, of those simple ideas.

(2) The second point, and the trivial paradox, is that the *General Theory* itself is built formally on the assumption of competition in the goods market. So much the worse for Keynes. That assumption got him into trouble right away. There was enough price deflation during the Depression that the assumption did not seem ridiculous on its face. But it led to the prediction that the real wage would be countercyclical, and it was soon pointed out that the world was not like that in actual fact. Keynes was quick to abandon the idea of perfect competition, and seemed to realize that his theory would make more sense without it. The history points to something else. There has been an occasional attempt to *identify* Keynesian ideas with monopolistic competition. In both contexts, it often turns out that output is "too small." But there is more than one way for output to be too small. I think monopolistic competition is a better context for understanding Keynesian ideas, but it is not a substitute for them nor another way of saying the same thing. A felt demand constraint is not the same thing as a "wrong" price.

The two chapters that follow in Part I (the Caffè Lectures) are intended to promote the idea that explicit modeling of imperfect competition in the product market will be good for macroeconomics, in two ways. First, it facilitates the accurate description and analysis of modes of behavior that correspond better to what we see in the course of macroeconomic fluctuations. The general shape of operating macro models might change a little, or a lot, or hardly at all. That is hard to guess in advance. Second, macroeconomics can be built on more realistic micro foundations, so consciences can rest easier. Thinking about behavior in imperfect markets – the need to form expectations about the location of demand curves, for instance – might suggest alternative aggregative relations to test, and might eventually lead to new ways of structuring empirically relevant macro models. The first chapter discusses some general implications of imperfectly competitive markets; the second provides one example of a macro model built on such foundations.

Part II, following the Caffé Lectures, reprints an earlier paper of mine on the role of imperfect competition in macroeconomics. The purpose of this chapter is not the detailed calculation of the government-spending multiplier, although that is what takes up most of the space. The particular result depends on the details of the model – they are special and might not carry over to other formulations. The real point is different. Nearly all attempts to incorporate monopolistic competition into aggregative models make use of the Dixit–Stiglitz formalization of the demand for a group of goods that are symmetrically imperfect substitutes for one another. That formalization deserves the attention it gets; it works very neatly.

For some purposes, however, I think the old competition-on-a-circle model, originally due to Harold Hotelling, has advantages. In the circle model, there is less symmetry; a firm has nearest neighbors, and it competes primarily with them. This set-up leads to a rather different picture of what it means for a new firm to enter (or, more generally, for new capacity to appear). In the Dixit–Stiglitz picture, a new firm produces a new product, competing symmetrically with all pre-existing products. In the Hotelling picture, a new firm has to force its way into a niche "between" two existing firms. In the first instance it competes primarily with them. They may in turn put some competitive pressure on their neighbors (and they on theirs). In real life it may take a long time for a new ($n$+1)-firm equilibrium to establish itself. In the meantime, the entrant and its particular rivals may suffer losses, may engage in predatory tactics, and will have to form expectations about the longer-run future, including expectations about rivals' beliefs and actions. I think that sort of focus may be a useful lead into the macroeconomics of "animal spirits," etc., and I have some ambition to develop the story further along that line.

The paper reprinted here as chapter 3 can be read as an easy introduction to the use of that framework for macroeconomics with imperfect competition. It is very special in its assumptions, and the particular results depend on those assumptions. The process of establishing a new equilibrium after a shock, which is where much of the interesting macro theory may lie, is not investigated. The story is pure comparative statics, comparing one equilibrium with another. But I hope this chapter points the way to a fruitful analytical setting for macroeconomics under imperfect competition.

# Part I

Federico Caffé Lectures

# 1

# Some macroeconomic implications of monopolistic competition

The subject of this and the next chapter might naturally be classified under the now familiar heading "micro foundations of macroeconomics." That would not be my preferred description, but I cannot claim that it is inappropriate. My substantive and methodological goals, however, are quite different from those that motivated the concern for micro foundations that erupted into consciousness about fifteen years ago and has shaped it since then, creating a distinctive school of thought.

Like other successful schools of thought, this one has made itself appear newer than it really is. Probably from the very beginning, theoretical arguments in macroeconomics have been explained and justified by microeconomic reasoning. The way you convince yourself and others that a particular macroeconomic relationship is sound is by arguing that it is plausible in terms of what we think we know about the behavior of households and business *and* that it fits the aggregative facts. That is how Keynes made his case for the consumption function and the marginal-efficiency schedule. (Remember: it is a "psychological law" of individual behavior that the marginal propensity to consume should be between zero and one.) Any textbook of macroeconomics, today or yesterday, follows the same route in motivating students.

So the current passion for micro foundations is not really trying to make that unassailable point. Its contribution has been to take the micro foundational point literally, too literally in my opinion. In their desire to insist that the only valid macro model is the exact aggregation of a micro model, the protagonists of the newer school have been led to favor two very narrow basic presumptions.

The first of these is a bias in favor of models populated by a single representative agent who lives forever, or perhaps by a large number of identical immortal agents. That device certainly solves the aggregation problem neatly, but at the cost of ignoring every problem that arises from the heterogeneity of households and firms, and that means, arguably, ignoring nearly everything that is interesting in macroeconomics. This presumption is not, however, part of my main concern and so I will not delve into it too deeply here.

The second presumption, and the one on which I want to focus, is that the microeconomy's markets are perfectly competitive. There is an irony here: you can find support for this assumption in the *General Theory* (1936). Keynes was generally predisposed to accept what he called the first fundamental postulate of classical economics, that the (real) wage is equal to the marginal product of labor, "subject, however, to the qualification that the equality may be disturbed, in accordance with certain principles, if competition and markets are imperfect." But he did not insist on the qualification and evidently regarded it as merely making the wage proportionally less than the marginal product of labor. A reader would not go wrong by taking it that, throughout the book, price is equal to marginal cost (or proportional to it). Indeed, when labor is the only variable factor of production, the two statements are equivalent. It suited his subversive purpose to argue as much as he could on the enemy's home ground.

But many modern Keynesians (including at least James Tobin and Paul Samuelson) have pointed out that the natural habitat of Keynesian economics is an environment of imperfect competition or monopolistic competition in which business firms have some control over their own prices. That is what I want to spell out in this first chapter. What advantages does a model based on predominantly imperfect competition hold out for macroeconomic theory and practice?

## Excess supply

In one respect, any general equilibrium model characterized by monopolistic competition will "look" a little Keynesian. There is always, in a certain sense, excess supply of goods. Every elementary student is taught that an imperfectly competitive firm does not have a supply curve, because it chooses its price endogenously; the price is not given by the market. So it cannot be quite right to describe such a firm as "off its supply curve." What one can say is that an imperfectly competitive firm would always be glad to produce and sell additional output at the current price. Of course it does not have that choice. In textbook language: price exceeds marginal cost at equilibrium, but marginal revenue is just equal to marginal cost.

The point of this elementary fact is that an increase in demand will have multiplier-like effects. An outward shift of the demand curve will increase profits, and the spending of the increment in profits (according to routine utility maximization) will shift the demand curve further, and so on. Even the familiar geometric series emerge naturally in such comparative-static calculations. The details will depend on the particular assumption maintained about the spending of monopoly profit. Profit may be lumped indiscriminately with other income, or may be saved in greater proportion than wages. In any case the economy will respond to demand shocks with a recognizable multiplier process. The full story is more complicated, however. Even in a simple general-equilibrium model, there will be offsetting effects on the cost side. The final outcome could be quite different.

My own inclination is to resist applying the "Keynesian" label to this pattern, but it is only a weak inclination. The multiplier process perhaps deserves the label, but the important thing in macroeconomics is not the elementary mechanics of the multiplier, but the reasons for its presence. The excess of price over marginal cost under imperfect competition means that policy-induced demand expansion can move the economy closer to ideal output. This possibility does not rest on any shortage of effective demand. Nevertheless, the work of Hart (1982), Mankiw (1988), Startz (1989), and Blanchard and Kiyotaki (1987) is certainly a step toward enriching the micro foundations of macroeconomics.

## "Menu costs"

The first idea that I want to describe may not be the most important, but it has the special merit of connecting directly to one standard interpretation of Keynesian macroeconomics. The original papers are by Akerlof and Yellen (1985) and by Mankiw (1985). (Here and elsewhere, references and guides to the literature will be found in the Bibliographical note appended to each chapter. See also the excellent survey article by Dixon and Rankin (1994), which lists further references.) I am not looking for the greatest generality of exposition, but rather the clearest intuition.

Think of a single producer of a differentiated product facing given cost conditions and a downward-sloping demand curve based on whatever expectations she has about the behavior of other producers. Her problem is to find the best price to charge. Profit, in other words, is a function of that price. Under the micro assumptions that have become standard, the profit function rises smoothly to a unique maximum – at the price that makes marginal revenue equal to marginal cost – and then descends smoothly at still higher prices. It is the smoothness that matters, and that follows from smooth demand and cost curves. For example, if the demand curve is linear and total costs are quadratic in output, then the profit function is quadratic in the price. So there is a unique profit-maximizing price. The key implication is that near the best price the loss in profit for any small error in price setting is second order, exactly quadratic in the case I mentioned and approximately quadratic in any smooth case. Small deviations from the best price entail *very* small consequences for the firm's profit.

Notice how important it is that the market be imperfectly competitive. For a perfect competitor, even a very small error in pricing has big consequences. If the price is set just a little too high, sales will drop off to zero. If the price is set a bit too low, the firm will be overwhelmed with orders that cannot be filled profitably. The loss in profits is approximately proportional to the error in setting the price. If this strikes you as an unlikely experience, it only means that you think perfect competition is an unlikely market form.

The interesting macroeconomic implication of this microeconomic observation is that imperfectly competitive firms may feel no pressure to change their prices when there are small fluctuations in demand or cost conditions. If there are even minor transaction costs involved in frequent price changes, it may well be optimal to keep prices fixed for long intervals in a slowly or slightly changing environment. This story goes under the name of "menu costs"; the reference is to the fact that the cost of printing new restaurant menus is the sort of friction that may keep restaurant prices fixed when market conditions change, as long as the change is not too large. That is a picturesque example, but the force of the theory comes from the likelihood that other sorts of costs are more important than the printing of new price lists: customers have to be informed; they may be irritated by frequent price changes; private information may be inadvertently communicated to rival sellers. Whatever its realism and significance, this is a story in which imperfectly competitive micro foundations lead to an endogenous theory of sticky prices. One of the standard textbook versions of Keynesianism can be made to rest on sticky wages and prices. Presumably this Keynesian model is made more respectable when its premise is shown to be compatible with optimization or near optimization.

The menu-cost theory is completed by another proposition. Although the individual firm's loss of profit from price inflexibility is second order, the loss in social welfare is first order: the ratio of social loss to private loss will be very large for small errors. A small reduction in aggregate demand that is ignored by most firms will cost each of them very little in foregone profit, maybe nothing at all in view of menu costs. But the fact that very many firms leave their prices "a little too high" and thus produce "a little too little" can add up to a significant first-order reduction in aggregate output. This is not a macro theory yet. It needs a lot of general equilibrium embellishment to become a complete theory, not much of which has been provided in the literature. But I mean it to serve only as a first example of the fact that imperfectly competitive micro foundations do not necessarily lead to the sort of Panglossian macroeconomics that has come to be associated with perfectly competitive, representative-agent models.

I should mention that the menu-cost model is only the tip of a small iceberg. A whole school of thought has emerged that calls itself "New Keynesian" and pursues a broad research program aimed at *deducing* price stickiness from more basic assumptions about transaction costs and uncertainty. (The implied contrast is from "Old Keynesians" who simply *assumed* prices to be sticky.) I think this is a worthwhile enterprise. It has produced quite a lot of interesting research, interesting even on purely microeconomic grounds, but with macroeconomic implications. I doubt, however, that this can be the main battlefield in the intellectual conflict between broadly "Classical" and broadly "Keynesian" views of the way the aggregate economy works and the way economic fluctuations are best to be interpreted.

My reasons for holding this view are not directly related to the theme discussed here; but they have some oblique relevance and may be worth stating fully. The presuppositions of a theory often determine the questions to which theory provides answers. (There is a well-known word game: here is the answer – what is the question?) The (new-) Classical approach to macroeconomics presupposes that observed events are tracing out the full competitive equilibrium of the underlying economy. That being so, only real things should matter for the real economy. Money should be a fairly transparent veil. The major problem the world presents to this theory is to explain why purely nominal disturbances seem to have real consequences. Protagonists of this view like to find answers that do not call into question the underlying theoretical presuppositions. The menu-cost model accepts the question and produces an answer that may open the way to Keynesian ideas.

To my mind the question, while interesting, is not so fundamental. The reason is that, as soon as one abandons the representative-agent-in-competitive-equilibrium framework as unnatural and implausible, it is easy to think of practical, everyday reasons for price stickiness. And then we know that nominal events will have real consequences. If I had to nominate a central question for macroeconomics, it would not be that one. I think I would revert to an older tradition in business-cycle theory and ask: when a modern industrial economy is struck by a real disturbance, like a sudden reduction in the perceived profitability of investment or a sudden increase in the propensity to save, why does it take so long to return to full-employment equilibrium? The menu-cost model does not provide an answer to this question.

## Quantity expectations

Now I turn to a second implication of imperfectly competitive market forms, one that also has implications for macroeconomic theory. A perfectly competitive firm needs to form expectations only about the market price of its products in order to make its decisions about employment and output. (Of course it also needs to know its costs, including input prices. That does not change the point I want to make, so I shall concentrate exclusively on the demand side.) Usually the price is a public fact; but that is only a little help to the firm, because it must try to predict the price some time in the future. A monopolistically competitive firm does not have to predict a price; it sets its own price. But it needs to know something different, more complicated, and probably more uncertain. It has to predict the location and shape of its demand curve.

The first thing to notice is that this is a *quantity* expectation, not a price expectation. This is why we so often observe firms paying for national economic forecasts and then for special analyses that try to work out the implications of a national forecast for a specific industry, or even for a part of an industry. (A separate industry has grown up to provide these forecasts and analyses.) In principle price forecasts could be derived in the same top-down way. My casual impression is that price forecasts are in fact less macroeconomics intensive than quantity forecasts.

The significant observation about the need for quantity forecasts is that it can quite easily lead to "strategic complementarities" across wide areas of the economy. (The standard discussion of this subject is by Cooper and John (1988).) The concept can be given a more abstract definition, but for our purposes it is enough to say that strategic complementarity arises when greater output or employment or resource-use by one sector of the economy *increases* the marginal profitability of output or employment or resource-use in another sector of the economy. The importance of strategic complementarity is that it gives rise to reaction functions that slope in the same direction. Suppose you were to produce more. If that increases the marginal profitability of output to me, then my best response will be to produce more. Thus the more I expect you to produce, the more I will produce. Symmetrically, the more you expect me to produce the more you will produce.

Reaction functions that slope in the same direction can obviously intersect more than once. Each intersection is a (Nash) equilibrium, a pair of decisions, one for me and one for you, each of which is a best response to the other and thus leads to no internal pressure for either of us to change. So strategic complementarity is a likely source of multiple equilibria. More than that, such collections of equilibria can easily turn out to be "Pareto-rankable"; one of them may be better than the other for both of us, or for all of us if other agents are involved.

So far this is just an interesting theoretical possibility. It becomes important for macroeconomics only if it captures something that we recognize as real and non-trivial in the macroeconomic world that we see. There are some suggestions along those lines to be found in the literature.

Perhaps the most straightforward is to be found in a paper by W. P. Heller (1986). Since it is a formal model, there are only two sectors in the economy. Each of them sells only to the workers (or other recipients of income) in the other. This sounds more artificial than it is: in a many-sector economy, no sector sells more than a negligible part of its output to its own workers and shareholders, so there is no possibility of a bootstrap operation that generates a significant increase in own-demand by producing more goods.

In this situation, each firm or sector must estimate the other firm's or sector's level of output in order to predict the position of its own demand curve. The more you produce, the more wages you will pay out, and the more income will be available to be spent on the goods I produce. Of course the world looks the same to you, only you have to predict my production decision. The stage is set for strategic complementarity, and Heller does all the technical work to show that there can easily be two equilibrium configurations. In one of them, each firm expects the other to decide on a high level of employment and output. Each therefore expects the demand curve for its own output to be strong. Each therefore decides on a high level of production. There is an equilibrium in which each sells what it expected to sell. Each firm's optimism is confirmed by the other's behavior.

There can also be another, lower-level, equilibrium. If each firm expects the other to produce a low ("recession") level of output, then each firm will find it best to produce a low level of output. In the low-level equilibrium, each firm's pessimistic expectations are confirmed by the other's behavior. There are no surprises and a low-level equilibrium exists under certain technical conditions.

A complete model would have to worry about equilibrium in the labor market, and perhaps elsewhere, but there is little doubt that it could all be arranged. Not only that, it could be arranged so that the high-output equilibrium is better than the low-output equilibrium for everybody involved, workers and managers in both firms or sectors. A self-confirming optimistic equilibrium is then better than a self-confirming pessimistic equilibrium. What conclusions should we draw from this exercise?

First of all, it strongly suggests the possibility of a macro model in which each of many sectors bases its decisions on a forecast of the aggregate economy. If each sector's or most sectors' expectations are optimistic, they will expand and together will bring about something very like a high-level equilibrium in the aggregate. A preponderance of pessimistic forecasts about the aggregate will lead most sectors to contract and the result may be a low-level aggregate equilibrium in which pessimism is confirmed and therefore reinforced.

Stories like this go back a long way: in the English-language literature, at least to D. H. Robertson and A. C. Pigou (1939) in the early part of this century. They were writing about business cycles. Here we are concerned with persistent equilibrium states.

The second thing to notice is that here, as with all multiple-equilibrium stories, it is very important to know something about the forces that lead the economy to "choose" one equilibrium configuration rather than another. That may spell the difference between prosperity and recession. The model itself has little to tell us on this score, except to hint that historical, accidental, sociological, and even psychological factors may play a role, and to remind us that one function of economic policy may be to help or induce the economy to "choose" a better rather than a worse equilibrium.

Finally, I want to remind you that this kind of story has a definite Keynesian air to it: not from the part of the *General Theory* that is most consistent with sticky wages, ISLM, and all that, but from the part that emphasizes "animal spirits" and the "state of long-term expectations" and that led an earlier generation to describe temporary expansionary policy as "priming the pump," as shifting the economy from a dead state to a live state that could reproduce itself without outside help if only it could once be achieved.

There is a quite different version of strategic complementarity in which the "you" and the "I" are not two firms or sectors of the economy, but two periods of time. It appears in a paper by Kiyotaki (1988) that is even more Keynesian in its structure. I shall describe this model in a cursory way, because it is not obscure and the underlying idea is much the same. Expectations about the aggregative state of the economy in the next period are the main determinant of investment expenditure in this period. So the more optimistic firms are about the next period, the more prosperous the aggregate economy will be in this period. That is not exactly a "reaction function" but it can serve the same purpose. Now there are many ways in which prosperity in this period can spill over positively into the next period. One possibility is that currently high incomes can generate a high level of consumption spending next period. (This is sometimes called a "Robertsonian" lag.) There are no doubt many other mechanisms. What matters is that optimism about the future should be self-confirming.

Once again, as Kiyotaki shows, there can be (at least) two equilibria. In one of them, optimism about tomorrow creates prosperity today and tomorrow and, quite possibly, sets the stage for further optimism and prosperity. In the other equilibrium, pessimism about tomorrow creates recession today and tomorrow and perhaps invites its continuation. I emphasize that this is an old story, appearing before the General Theory as well as in it. The difference is that there it is given precise expression in a formal model.

I will mention one more way of producing multiple Pareto-rankable equilibria. It is due to my colleague Peter Diamond (1982) and rests on search theory.

Suppose that production and employment are limited by the producers' uncertainty that they will be able to sell the resulting output, or more accurately to exchange it for someone else's output. Suppose that the uncertainty arises from the need literally to search for a partner in exchange. The longer it takes to find one, the less profitable the production-exchange enterprise will be. It is easier to find a partner and make a sale when many other producers are searching (the market is "thick") than when there are only a few (and the market is "thin"). This is already interesting: it says that each act of production creates a positive trading externality (a "thick-market" externality). By adding one more potential exchange partner to the market, each act of production makes everyone else's enterprise more profitable.

It is intuitive – and of course it can be worked out in detail – that this sort of economy can have two or more equilibria.

In a high-level equilibrium many firms or agents produce; since there are many of them, they make sales easily and therefore profitably. The profit justifies their original willingness to produce. In a depressed equilibrium there are few decisions to produce. The market is thin; exchanges are few and far between and therefore relatively unprofitable. No one regrets having held production to a low level. There could, of course, be any number of such equilibria in which the level of production actually undertaken is exactly justified by the observed difficulty of making a sale. Moreover it is pretty obvious that higher-output equilibria are better than lower-output equilibria. (Even the best equilibrium may have an inefficiently low level of production, because of the trading externality. But that is not the point I want to emphasize.)

Each of these strategic-complementarity stories rests on the need for imperfectly competitive firms to base production or investment decisions on quantity expectations. In principle, something similar could occur with price expectations, and thus perhaps under perfect competition. It is interesting, however, that the tradition in economics has gone the other way. The more usual story is that widespread expectations of a high price lead to overproduction, flooding the market, and the realization of a low price. The more usual outcome is a cobweb cycle, not persistent multiple equilibria. It is, however, a partial-equilibrium story.

## Increasing returns to scale

The existence of monopolistic competition allows us to model an economy with some degree of increasing returns to scale. The typical firm may produce along a falling or U-shaped unit cost curve. As long as the marginal-revenue curve is falling fast enough to cut the falling marginal-cost curve from above, the firm's profit-maximization problem is well defined. It is a two-way street. Just as monopolistic competition permits equilibrium with increasing returns to scale, some degree of increasing returns to scale is necessary to make sense of monopolistic competition. Unless there is some minimum efficient scale of production, it is hard to imagine where the firm's monopoly power can come from. (Martin Weitzman (1982) has argued persuasively that this sort of situation is necessary for any sort of unemployment equilibrium to persist. If tiny bits of unemployed resources could organize themselves into tiny, but efficient, producing units, they would do so and thus employ themselves.) My goal now is to show you that the very same structure leads naturally and inevitably to a specific role for "animal spirits" very much in the Keynesian vein.

From Chamberlin on, any large-group model of a monopolistically competitive industry in equilibrium automatically generates a distinction between the long run and the short run. In the short run, the population of firms is given. Each of them earns whatever profit it can, depending on the economic environment. If demand conditions are favorable, most or all firms will have positive profits; when demand conditions are weak, some or most or all of them may make losses. Profits will generally rise when firms' perceived demand curves shift upward and fall when demand curves shift downward, unless something very peculiar is happening to the elasticity of demand.

This sort of model is usually completed by a natural entry condition. When profits are generally high, new entrants are attracted, and entry will lower profits all around. When profits are negative, or low, or below "normal," there may be exit from the industry. If sub-normal profits persist, some incumbent firms will surely leave. Exit will tend to raise the profits of survivors. Long-run equilibrium rules when the number of firms in the industry is such that profits fluctuate around the normal level. Then neither entry nor exit occurs on an appreciable scale. (There is no harm in setting the "normal" level of profit at zero. The normal return to capital and reward to entrepreneurship are then included among the costs of production.)

Now imagine such an industry in a *short-run* equilibrium, with the average firm earning profits at some moderate level. Will entry take place? In discussing this question I allow myself to go outside the formal model and argue in common-sense terms.

Entry is necessarily a risky business, with a real possibility of irreversible loss. Because of increasing returns to scale, a new firm must achieve a non-trivial size in order to have any hope of success. This fact can have two important consequences. The first is that a substantial, lumpy, initial investment may be required to establish a potentially viable firm. Much of this stake may be irrecoverable if the new firm fails. The second consequence is that the entering firm, once it is established, will surely lose money as long as its output remains small.

To be successful, the firm must carve out a market niche for itself. It must win market share away from some of the existing firms who are currently meeting all of the market demand. The niche can take several forms. It can be a geographical market area, literally or figuratively, as when a new supermarket locates itself between two existing stores, or when a clothing manufacturer aims to penetrate a well-defined segment of the market, like young, single, professional males. A market niche can equally well be defined in "product space." The new firm finds a set of product characteristics that is not now saturated by an established producer, and hopes to make its living there.

However the entering firm defines its market niche, it will have one or more "nearest neighbors" from whom it must capture an appreciable quantity of sales in order to survive. The established firms will naturally resist by cutting price, increasing their advertising budgets, bringing out new products, or doing any of the things imperfectly competitive firms do in these circumstances. The entering firm is very likely to suffer losses at first (and inflict losses or reduced profits on its rivals in the industry). This initial period may actually last for quite a while.

If the entering firm survives, what reward can it look forward to? According to the theory it can look forward to a stream of profits, slightly lower than firms were earning before the current entry episode took place. Eventually profits will be approximately "normal," with occasional periods of sub-normal profits or losses, and occasional booms with super-normal profits. Sometimes, obviously, the story may be different, especially if the new firm is built around a technological innovation. But often enough the story will be something like the one I have told.

It does not seem far-fetched to say that entry will occur when animal spirits – optimism, aggressiveness, risk tolerance, optimism – are favorable. Otherwise many potential entrants will hang back. To use another Keynesian phrase, one could say that the state of long-term expectations governs the likelihood of entry corresponding to any given current degree of profitability in industry. It would be easy to add similar remarks about the attitudes of potential suppliers of credit.

Following tradition, I have been speaking of entry as if it always meant the appearance of a new firm. A macroeconomist will notice that everything I have said about "entry" applies equally well to "investment." What really matters is the appearance of new *capacity*. It could just as well represent cost-reducing or product-enhancing investment. It could just as well represent additional capacity for an existing firm. The important thing is that additions to capacity should be lumpy and should have to fight for market share with rivals. In this interpretation, what Chamberlin would describe as free entry, a macroeconomist would describe as a high elasticity of investment with respect to current or prospective future profitability. What we have really constructed is a theory in which animal spirits – but not only animal spirits – drives investment. The state of long-term expectations matters, but so does the general economic environment, especially the current and expected level of aggregate demand.

I believe that this is a substantively interesting and relevant model. My point is not to develop it in detail, but just to demonstrate how easy and how liberating it is to find micro foundations for Keynesian macroeconomics, and indeed how much more plausible those micro foundations are than the more usual representative-agent, Arrow–Debreu stories that preoccupy the various versions of new-Classical macroeconomics.

It may be worth pointing out that the particular story I have just been describing can easily give rise to many different equilibria, depending on the essentially exogenous state of long-term expectations. This is pretty transparent and I do not think it earns much credit for Keynesian economics. It may nevertheless capture something intuitive and real about our economy.

## Final remarks

A brief and incomplete survey like this cannot be expected to imply anything specific about the everyday world. Instead it is intended to provide some hints about the making of macroeconomic theories. I will get right to the point. I think that economists have been scared away from Keynesian-sounding theories and Keynesian-sounding conclusions during the past fifteen years or so. The problem is not that these now unfashionable theories cannot be made to fit the facts; they are considerably better than the currently fashionable theories in that respect. Economists have been frightened away by the belief or fear that those Keynesian-sounding ideas are incompatible with the micro foundations of the subject. We tend to be very respectful of the intellectual status of our science, as we ought to be. None of us – to repeat an old slogan – wants to be guilty of teaching macroeconomics on Tuesday and Thursday that is logically incompatible with the microeconomics we teach on Monday and Wednesday. I have been trying to convince you that it is more likely the Monday and Wednesday syllabus that needs revision.

A world whose normal market form is monopolistic competition does seem to be the natural habitat of Keynesian macroeconomics. (I will call it that from now on instead of using the awkward circumlocution "Keynesian-sounding." I adopted that at first just to underline the fact that I have no interest in ideological purity or the preservation of Keynes's specific ideas and beliefs.) Getting away from the neat and tractable world of perfect competition does seem to open up possibilities that sound very Keynesian. It may be worth remembering that his own casual acceptance of competitive assumptions got Keynes into trouble right away, by leading him to assert that real wages should behave counter cyclically, falling in upswings and rising in downswings. When it was pointed out, as early as 1937, that the facts were otherwise, Keynes was quite happy to recant.

The theme of this chapter has been that imperfectly competitive micro foundations seem to lead quite naturally, even inevitably, to concepts and ideas that are commonplace in the Keynesian tradition.

(1) To begin with, there is even some warrant for price stickiness. The menu-cost literature suggests that the optimal response of imperfectly competitive firms to small shocks to aggregate demand could be to leave prices unchanged. The resulting fluctuations in output can have significant welfare effects. This particular reason for imperfect price flexibility is in addition to the less formal argument about customer markets advanced by Arthur Okun a decade ago. (Okun's ideas could probably be formalized in game-theoretic terms as a form of rent sharing.)

Since I have emphasized the possible multiplicity of

equilibria in this lecture, I should point out that the menu-cost story could be thought of as a demonstration of the possibility of a whole interval – though perhaps only a narrow one – of macroeconomic equilibria. Even if one might not care to push it quite that far, the theory provides the raw material for a story about relatively slow return to an equilibrium disturbed by a small shock to aggregate demand. Menus do get changed, though infrequently.

(2) The next result was a way of making the idea of underemployment equilibrium respectable. (There is a qualification here that I will come to in a moment.) Sellers with market power must base their own decision making on expectations about the behavior of other sellers, or about the state of the aggregate economy. That being so, one of the defining characteristics of an equilibrium must be the requirement that the underlying expectations not be systematically invalidated by the outcome. The work of Heller (1986), Diamond (1982), and others shows that it is then possible to have more than one macroeconomic equilibrium, with self-confirming expectations, even when higher-level equilibria are clearly better, actually Pareto-better, than lower-level equilibria. It is possible in this way to make good on Keynes's unfulfilled promise to demonstrate the possibility of equilibrium with less than full employment.

Now I must come to the qualification just mentioned. Anyone who wishes to talk about equilibrium employment and unemployment needs to embed the discussion in a fully fledged model of the labor market. I have stayed deliberately away from that subject here. There is a large and complex literature on macroeconomic aspects of the labor market. I have contributed to it and discussed it elsewhere. I cannot survey it now. In principle, therefore, I have been talking about equilibria with underproduction rather than under-employment. But there is no real doubt that the two can be combined.

(3) The third Keynesian idea that surfaced quite naturally in the context of monopolistic competition was "animal spirits." I have always felt uncomfortable with this notion because it is such a convenient *deus ex machina*, capable of being trundled on and off the macroeconomic stage at one's convenience. I hope to have made a plausible case that some such concept is bound to arise as soon as entry and capacity expansion are embedded in the short-run and long-run equilibria of a monopolistically competitive industry. This conclusion cannot be dodged by invoking "rational expectations" because the things that have to be anticipated include the anticipations and behavior of other agents. In the repeated-game context there is no universally acceptable way out of multiplicity of equilibria.

It is in the nature of imperfect competition in a world with increasing returns to scale that the state of long-term expectations should influence and sometimes dominate the propensity to invest. One can then tell a good story about high-level and low-level equilibria, with the economy capable of getting stuck in the wrong one. This is Keynes's case for activist policy, but I can leave its elaboration to the reader as an exercise. The thing to keep in mind is that these possibilities are now an *implication* of micro foundations, not a violation of them.

## Bibliographical note

Dixon and Rankin's clear and comprehensive article "Imperfect Competition and Macroeconomics: A Survey" (*Oxford Economic Papers* 46 (1994) 171–90) had not appeared when the Caffé Lectures were given. There is some overlap, but the article and the lecture are mostly complementary. Dixon and Rankin are more interested than I in the formal properties of the basic models, and in particular in figuring out which characteristics give rise to which properties. My goal, has been to motivate and justify the use of imperfect competition as a base for macro models, by showing that a lot of interesting and relevant things can happen that are excluded or suppressed by the assumption of perfect competition. For instance, Dixon and Rankin's discussion of the effectiveness or ineffectiveness of monetary policy in a model with imperfect competition seems less interesting to me, although it is worthwhile to get it straight. We all know lots of reasons why monetary policy bites on real output in the short-to-medium run. The main problem is to make these perfectly sound reasons respectable within the tradition of economics. Dixon and Rankin provide an extensive bibliography, so I can be very selective here.

Oliver Hart started the analytical ball rolling with "A Model of Imperfect Competition with Keynesian Features," *Quarterly Journal of Economics* 97 (1982) 109–38 (hereafter *QJE*). The phrase "with Keynesian features," like my own "Keynesian-sounding," points to the fact that these models are not doing exactly what Keynes had in mind, for which they are none the worse. See also G. Mankiw, "Imperfect Competition and the Keynesian Cross," *Economics Letters* 26 (1988) 68–74; R. Startz, "Monopolistic Competition as a Foundation for Keynesian Macroeconomic Models," *QJE* 104 (1989) 737–52; O. Blanchard and N. Kiyotaki, "Mono-polistic Competition and the Effects of Aggregate Demand," *American Economic Review* 77 (1987) 647–66.

The best place to study the menu-cost model is G. Akerlof and J. Yellen, "A Near-Rational Model of the Busi-ness Cycle with Wage and Price Inertia," *QJE* 100 (supp. 1985) 823–38; and G. Mankiw, "Small Menu Costs and Large Business Cycles: A Macroeconomic Model,' *QJE* 100 (1985) 529–37.

The "New-Keynesian" perspective is given a forceful statement in L. Ball and G. Mankiw, "A Sticky-Price Mani-festo" (Carnegie-Rochester Conference Series on Public Policy, vol. 41, 1994, 127–57). The two-volume anthology edited by G. Mankiw and D. Romer, *New Keynesian Eco-*

*nomics*, MIT Press, 1991, contains many of the essential papers, including some cited here.

"Strategic complementarity" takes many forms relevant to macroeconomics. It is not a theory or a model, but a common feature of many models. The papers I used in this lecture are: R. Cooper and A. John, "Coordinating Coordination Failures in Keynesian Models," *QJE* 83 (1988) 441–63; W. P. Heller, "Coordination Failures Under Complete Markets with Applications to Effective Demand," in W. Heller, R. Starr, and D. Starrett (eds.), *Equilibrium Analysis: Essays in Honor of K. J. Arrow*, II, Cambridge University Press, 1986; P. Diamond, "Aggregate Demand Management in Search Equilibrium," *Journal of Political Economy* 90 (1982) 881–94; N. Kiyotaki, "Multiple Expectational Equilibria under Monopolistic Competition," *QJE* 103 (1988) 695–713. It is worth looking at the ideas of Robertson and Pigou; a summary can be found in G. Haberler's classic *Prosperity and Depression* (League of Nations, 1939), chapter 6 on "psychological" theories.

For customer markets, I would recommend A. Okun's *Prices and Quantities* (Brookings Institution, 1981) and I. McDonald, *Inflation and Unemployment* (Blackwell, 1990). A very important recent contribution is Alan S. Blinder, Elie R. D. Canetti, David E. Lebow, and Jeremy B. Rudd, *Asking about Prices: A New Approach to Understanding Price Stickiness*, New York, Russell Sage Foundation, 1988.

My own paper "Monopolistic Competition and the Multiplier," reprinted as chapter 3 in this volume, was inspired by M. Weitzman, "Increasing Returns and the Foundations of Unemployment Theory," *Economic Journal* 92 (1982) 787–804. I like the Hotelling model of monopolistic competition on a circle precisely because it is a big help in visualizing the entry decision discussed in chapter 1. The same real problem can be squeezed into the Dixit–Stiglitz framework, but in that form it is easier to overlook. Some years ago, I developed this "animal spirits" argument a lot further, and incorporated it in two Mitsui Lectures I gave at the University of Birmingham in 1985. Subsequently, I found that I had botched one small piece of the story I told then – the error had nothing to do with the animal-spirits idea – and I never got around to fixing the lectures for publication. At least not yet.

Robin Marris has produced a complete general-equilibrium model based on monopolistic competition, in the form of a computer simulation program. See *Reconstructing Keynesian Economics with Imperfect Competition* (Edward Elgar, 1991). His instinct is probably right and mine wrong and old fashioned; but I find this close dependence on the computer screen less satisfying (intellectually, I mean) than older modes of theory. I like to see computer simulations after I think I understand the way a model works. Nevertheless Marris makes a powerful case for the affinity of Keynesian economics to imperfectly competitive market forms.

Just recently, Dennis Carlton has produced "A Critical Assessment of the Role of Imperfect Competition in Macroeconomics" (NBER Working Paper 5782, October 1996). He dwells carefully and accurately on a point I made in the Introduction and in the foregoing chapter: the increase in output (and the accompanying multiplier-like process) that arises in imperfectly competitive equilibrium after an exogenous injection of demand is not the same thing as the analogous increase in output in a Keynesian model. The first rests on an initial gap between price and marginal cost; the second does not, but instead activates initially idle resources. Carlton makes the illuminating comparison between the role of market power in the first case and the role of tax wedges between price and marginal cost in an otherwise competitive economy. The difference between the two cases is the difference between "Harberger triangles" and "Okun gaps." The rest of this interesting paper speaks to issues other than the ones discussed here.

# 2

## A Macroeconomic Model with Imperfect Competition

I have argued that many of the characteristic features of Keynesian (or Keynesian-sounding) models of the aggregate economy have a natural affinity with the microeconomics of any imperfectly competitive system of markets. That does not mean, however, that anyone is now entitled to write down a traditional ISLM model on the automatic presumption that it has sound micro foundations. It is still necessary to pass from some set of plausible micro assumptions to a corresponding macro model which may or may not look like some familiar construct.

What does it mean to say that a particular macro model "corresponds" to certain micro assumptions? One possible methodological decision is to insist that a valid macro model must be an exact aggregation of the corresponding micro-economy. Presumably that is what leads to the sort of aggregate economics I have been criticizing: a single representative agent maximizing an infinite-time utility function subject only to competitive market constraints, with informational, technological, and other assumptions that guarantee that a single price-taking firm will exactly carry out the optimizing agent's wishes. If that is the best that can be done, then I think the cost of the methodological commitment is much too high. That should not be surprising; the methodological commitment seems to be much too narrow anyway.

As an alternative, I would be quite content with a macro model that could be described as "loosely abstracted" from particular micro assumptions. All I mean by the phrase is that an acceptable macro model should look as if it could naturally arise from or otherwise represent a fully specified microeconomy with certain characteristics of market structure. Obviously no such process can provide sure protection against aggregation bias. The question may have to be investigated case by case; but that does not strike me as a bad thing.

In this chapter I would like to illustrate what I mean by giving an example of such a model. I am not suggesting that this is the right model, even less that it is a model that can be directly applied to interpret current economic events in your country or mine. It is, however, a model "loosely abstracted" from a microeconomic model built on monopolistically competitive foundations. It is intended just to exemplify the sorts of features a macro model might inherit from its microeconomic parent if it were not rooted in perfect competition. Some of these features are closely related to those I described as "Keynesian-sounding" in the previous chapter.

This model and its microeconomic ancestor were developed during my long collaboration with Professor Frank Hahn, of Cambridge and the University of Siena. The microeconomic model from which it is "loosely abstracted" will be described in the joint work we are hoping to finish. Its details are not needed here. Rough analogy is all that I want to claim and all that I think macroeconomics needs to claim.

There is one major excuse I must make; and it is only fair that I should make it up front, to avoid false pretenses. I mentioned in the first chapter the obvious warning that any model of unemployment equilibrium has to include a labor market that operates in some essentially non-Walrasian way. That is just a matter of definition. Persistent excess supply is inconsistent with Walrasian equilibrium. Several ways of modeling a non-clearing labor market are now available in the literature. I have no need at this stage to choose among them. So I shall just assume, without any argument, that the nominal wage is rigid, at least so long as employment and unemployment stay within certain specified bounds. There is no force that automatically works to eliminate excess supply of or excess demand for labor. I shall go about my business in connection with the goods market and merely take it for granted that some of the equilibria I find involve unemployment rates within the range that will leave the nominal wage passive. I can talk about unemployment in this model, but I have not earned the right to talk about it seriously. There is no doubt, however, that the model could be fixed up with a fully specified non-Walrasian labor market. The Hahn and Solow (1995) book goes considerably further in that direction.

## Background assumptions

There are two produced goods in this model economy, a consumer good and an investment good; and there are two factors of production, labor and capital, the latter being the stock of investment goods. Just to simplify calculations, the investment-goods sector is made to be quite primitive. Investment goods are produced by labor alone, under constant returns, and they disappear completely after one period of use. Each of these simplifications achieves a different purpose. The first one is harmless. It just cuts off one chain of minor general-equilibrium effects, the one that works through changes in factor intensity in the investment-goods sector. This assumption could be relaxed with no greater cost than a lot of algebra. Once it is made, however, the technology might as well exhibit constant returns, and the natural consequence is that the market for investment goods is modeled as perfectly competitive. The effects of monopolistic competition will be felt through the consumer-goods sector.

The other assumption, that capital goods wear out in one period, is more significant. It is made because there is no good alternative. If capital goods are very durable, then either one must assume perfect long-distance foresight, which strikes me as self-defeating for macroeconomics, or one is reduced to some more or less plausible but arbitrary investment function. I do not know of any convincing but tractable theory of the valuation of durable capital goods when the future is confused. There is a place for rational expectations models, but this is not it. The one-period lifetime for capital dodges the issue, while still allowing investment decisions to be made in partial ignorance of the location of next period's demand curve. I will just assume that investment decisions are made on the basis of point expectations about next period's demand. The expectations may turn out to be false, but by then the investment is committed. This is a serious deficiency in any theory that would like to be more or less Keynesian. It rules out one main channel by which the "state of long-term expectations" exerts an influence on short- and medium-run equilibrium. (That deficiency might perhaps be patched up.)

On the household side, I shall adopt the common assumption that there is a fixed, inelastic supply of labor. On the business-cycle time scale, that is probably an innocuous convention. I have never been able to convince myself of the utility of models in which induced variations in the supply of labor play a significant short-run role. Spending decisions are related to income with a Robertsonian lag. Dividends are paid out at the end of each period after actual profits and losses have been realized. For simplicity, we might just as well assume that wages are paid at the same time. At that instant, households hold all the purchasing power and they allocate it between consumption expenditure and saving in the following period.

This decision too involves some uncertainty. At the moment when households decide how much to spend and how much to save, they do not know what the nominal price of consumer goods will be in the next period. Neither do they know what rate of return they will be able to earn on their savings. The model assumes that they form point expectations about both of those unknowns, expectations which may be disappointed when events unfold. It would be possible to make the model fully stochastic; but at this stage I think it is better simply to treat point expectations as parameters. One can then easily ask how events would have been affected if households and firms had held different expectations at the beginning of the period. That is an important question in macroeconomics, and an important test of a model.

If expectations turn out to be contradicted by events, the resulting situation is at best a "temporary" equilibrium. It will not repeat itself, because expectations will change. How they will change is, as you know, a matter for discussion. The "rational expectations" school thinks there is only one serious answer permissible. It would condemn any mechanical process of the formation and adaptation of expectations as *ad hoc*. I have occasionally reflected that it is better to be *ad hoc* than to be wrong. For my purposes, however, it does not matter. The important observation is that any temporary equilibrium will be temporary. One of the required characteristics of a medium-run or persistent equilibrium is that the expectations that gave rise to it should be confirmed by events. That can be checked out without the need for a theory of the formation of expectations.

Much of the action in this model takes place in the consumer-goods sector. Consumer goods are produced by capital and labor under conditions of increasing returns to scale, but with diminishing returns to each factor separately. The typical producing firm is a monopolistic competitor in its output market, but it believes that it can hire all the labor it wants at a given nominal wage. (As long as the outcome involves an unemployment rate in the passive range I mentioned earlier, this belief turns out to be true.)

The firm sees itself as competing symmetrically with other

firms producing imperfect substitutes. It has to forecast the *level* of its demand curve in the coming period. That will depend primarily on the aggregate income of the whole economy and will eventually be determined by the uncoordinated actions of firms and households taken together. Whatever the *level* of the demand curve facing each firm, it is assumed to have a constant relative-price *elasticity*, known to the firm. Here is another point of entry for expectations. The firm has to forecast the general price level for consumer goods. Its own sales will depend on the price it sets, relative to this price level. Given its expectations about the level of the demand curve and the average price set by competitors, the firm chooses its own price and production plan to maximize something. But to maximize what?

To answer that question, we must first understand the capital market, the institutional arrangement within which the firm finances its investment spending. Our story goes like this. Investment goods last for one period only. The nominal price of a machine is easy to calculate. Suppose it takes $q$ units of labor to make a machine; from constant returns and competition it follows that the price of a machine is $q$ times the nominal wage. Once it has decided how many machines to buy, the firm finances their purchase by selling one-period equity securities to households. A unit of equity entitles its owner to a proportionate share in the *surplus* achieved by the firm during the period in which the corresponding machines are used. The surplus of the firm is its gross margin, the amount by which its sales revenue exceeds its wage bill. The suppliers of equity are the residual claimants to the surplus of the firm. Once it has raised capital and bought machines, the firm will try to maximize that surplus.

Yes, but how much capital will the firm raise? How much investment will it do? The demand for equities comes from households who are saving from incomes already earned, and also from cash balances already in their possession.

That total of purchasing power will be divided into three parts: consumption spending, holdings of transaction balances, and purchases of equity. It seems safe to assume that households will place a larger fraction of their resources in equity the higher the rate of return they expect to earn. So the demand for equity is an increasing function of expected surplus to cost of investment.

Equity shares are supplied by firms in the consumer-goods sector. The firm holds expectations about its demand curve in the coming period. For each possible number of machines purchased, it would hire enough labor to maximize its surplus, conditional on those expectations. So for each hypothetical number of machines, the firm can calculate its expected (gross) rate of return, the ratio of expected surplus to the cost of the machines. As long as the degree of increasing returns to scale is not too great, a larger investment in machines will go with a lower expected rate of return. The capital market clears when firms are financing just enough investment so that the rate of return they expect to earn with that much investment will induce households, if they share those expectations, to buy just enough equity to finance that very investment.

In the end, things may not turn out as planned. A particular firm may have overestimated or underestimated the average price charged by competitors. It may have been excessively optimistic or pessimistic about the state of the market. It may achieve a bigger or smaller surplus than it had expected. Whatever the surplus turns out to be, it is paid out at the end of the period to the equity owners. The return on their investment may thus be bigger or smaller than they had anticipated when they bought the shares. It might be interesting to work out what possibilities arise when firms and their shareholders have different expectations about the likely profitability of the firm; but Hahn and I have assumed that they hold their expectations in common, right or wrong.

This is a very limited model; it cannot possibly answer a

lot of practical questions about macroeconomics. But it is pretty clearly "loosely abstracted" from a micro model; it allows for increasing returns to scale and for the imperfect competition that inevitably accompanies increasing returns to scale. This model is meant to answer one simple but general question: what sorts of possibilities are opened up for macroeconomics by imperfectly competitive micro foundations? My next task is to formulate this model in a handful of straightforward interpretable equations. Afterwards we can see if the equilibria of the model have anything special or interesting about them.

## For example: a model

It is enough if there is only one firm in the consumption-goods sector. At the beginning of year $t$ it anticipates a demand curve of the form $z_t^* D(p_t/P_t^*)$. The firm expects aggregate real consumer demand to be $z^*$, and it expects the price level of consumer goods to be $P^*$. If it chooses its own price $p$, it expects its share of the market to be $D(p/P^*)$. If $p = p^*$ (as in a symmetric equilibrium), the market will be equally shared; so $D(1) = 1$, or $= 1/j$ if there are $j$ firms. When necessary, I will assume $D$ to have constant elasticity $\eta > 1$.

The production function of the firm says that its output in any year is $k^\tau f(n)$, where $k$ is the stock of capital, $n$ is the labor–capital ratio, and $\tau > 1$. This function is homogeneous of degree $\tau$ and thus exhibits increasing returns to scale; $f(n)$ can be any increasing function that allows diminishing returns to each factor separately.

As described earlier, once the firm has purchased $k$ units of capital, its objective is to maximize the surplus of revenue over its wage bill, given the expected position of the demand curve. This leads in the normal way to two equations

$$k_t^\tau f(n_t) = z_t^* (p_t/P_t^*)^{-\eta} \tag{1}$$
$$\alpha k_t^{\tau-1} f'(n_t) = W/p_t \tag{2}$$

where $\alpha = \dfrac{\eta - 1}{\eta}$ is the ratio of marginal revenue to price. The first of these insures that planned output and planned price lie on the expected demand curve. The second sets the planned marginal revenue product of labor equal to the nominal wage. Both are entirely traditional.

Now let us turn to the capital market, where the firm finances its acquisition of capital goods by selling claims to the surplus achieved by use of those capital goods. Households buy these shares in anticipation of a gross rate of return $R_t^*$ which is defined by

$$p_t k_t^\tau f(n_t) = Wn_t k_t + R_t^* qwk_t \tag{3}$$

where $Wq$ is the nominal price of a unit of investment goods and $nk$ is the labor input in year $t$, by definition. There is an immediate payoff to the simplicity of this formulation: (2) and (3) imply that

$$R_t^* = q^{-1}\left(\frac{f(n_t)}{\alpha f'(n_t)} - n_t\right) = q^{-1}g(n_t). \tag{4}$$

It is easily checked that $g(n)$ is an increasing function; indeed if the production function is Cobb–Douglas, $g(n)$ is just proportional to $n$.

One technical condition has to be added to make sure that marginal revenue always cuts marginal cost from above when both are varied by varying the input of capital. The necessary stipulation is that $\alpha\tau < 1$. This condition turns out to imply that more favorable expectations about demand and higher expected prices for competitors both induce the firm to lower its own planned price. But of course it also invests more and plans higher employment and output. Both conclusions, one a little strange and the other very straightforward, follow from increasing returns to scale.

One way to think about equation (3) is to say that it gives the supply prices of equities: $R^*$ is the gross rate of return the firm can afford to pay if the environment is such as to induce it to undertake a certain amount of investment and employment (and production and price). The demand side of the market comes from the saving and portfolio decisions of households.

I have already surveyed the course of events. At the very start of the year $t$, households have spendable resources in the amount $S_{t-1}$, say, made up of three components. The first is $P_{t-1}Y_{t-1}$, last year's sales by the consumption-goods sector. Part of this has just been paid out as wages and the rest as profits to equity owners, but I am lumping both forms of income together. The second component of $S_{t-1}$ is $qWk_{t-1}$, which represents the wages paid out last year by the sector producing investment goods. This sector generates no profits, because it operates under constant returns and perfect competition. The last component of $S_{t-1}$ is $M_{t-1}$, the cash balances held by households throughout year $t-1$. There is room for embellishment in all this, but that would take me away from the main line of exposition.

Now let $\sigma$ be the fraction of their spendable resources that households choose to invest in equities. It combines the results of portfolio decisions and saving decisions. Hundreds of economists have thought and written about the way this fraction is determined; and there are probably more theories than there are economists in that collection. In our longer work, Frank Hahn and I have embedded the determination of $\sigma$ in a standard overlapping-generations model and we have done the standard derivation of a life-cycle model. It will do no violence to the tradition if we simply imagine that $\sigma$ is an increasing function of $R^*$. The higher the rate of return expected on the capital market, the larger is the fraction of their available resources that households will commit to equities. This can hardly be the whole story, of course. Since the only alternative is cash, price-level expectations must play a role. But I am not about to develop a model of continuing inflation; on the contrary, I am going to consider stationary states in a moment. So I think it will be reasonable if I set the demand for equities equal to $\sigma(R^*)S$.

Then the capital market clears when this is just equal to the nominal amount of finance required by firms. Thus

$$qWk_t = \sigma(R_t^*)S_{t-1} = \sigma(R_t^*)(P_{t-1}Y_{t-1} + qWk_{t-1} + M_{t-1}). \quad (5)$$

It may seem strange that an "expected" rate of return is determined in a market. Part of the strangeness comes from the simplifying assumption that firms and households share the same expectations. But in fact the realized rate of return in year $t$ may turn out to be different from $R_t^*$. The capital market clears on the basis of what is inside the heads of the participants.

At this stage, only the demand for cash balances has been left hanging. In the micro model from which this macro model is "loosely abstracted," tradition insists that the demand for cash balances be strictly accounted for. We have worked it all out under the hypothesis that there is a partial cash-in-advance constraint: every purchase to be completed within a period requires that a given fraction of its nominal value be paid out in the form of an initial deposit in money. You may suggest that the phrase "cash in advance" does not constitute a theory, and I will agree. On the other hand, I am merely complying with a tradition, and the tradition appears to be satisfied by the phrase. The truth is that we all have a sound intuition about the reasons why rational agents should hold non-interest-bearing cash when they could be holding an equal value of short-dated securities. It is just messy – and fundamentally irrelevant – to go to the trouble of modeling that intuition. To do so would almost certainly require a fully stochastic approach. All that is legitimately the subject of a useful research program, but I do not think that macroeconomics can wait for its completion. For present purposes, I feel comfortable with the unsurprising assumption that households plan to hold cash balances in year $t$ equal to a fraction $L(R^*)$ of their expected expenditures, namely $P^*C^*$.

Since the *ex ante* budget identity says that $S_{t-1}$ is exhausted by the sum of consumption spending, purchases of equity, and planned cash balances, the model economy will satisfy

$$\left[1 + L(R_t^*)\right]P_t^* C_t^* = \left[1 - \sigma(R_t^*)\right]S_{t-1}.$$

There is still one major piece of tidying-up to do. When events actually unfold in year $t$, expectations will generally turn out to be invalidated. Firms and households will have made errors of judgment. In that sense the outcome will be only a  temporary equilibrium. Even if planned transactions turn out to be mutually inconsistent, some collection of consistent transactions will eventually take place. But what will they be?

I will tell the story I have in mind, without going to the trouble of writing down all the equations. I shall assume that employment, investment, production, and stock-market decisions are irrevocably committed at the very beginning of year $t$. So firms come into year $t$ with a given quantity of perishable output already produced. Households find themselves in year $t$ with a certain amount of purchasing power, namely $S_{t-1} - qWk_t$. Firms have no choice but to sell what they have produced, at whatever price it will bring. In other words, they supply all they have inelastically. Households divide their remaining resources between consumption spending and cash balances in such a way that actual cash balances is the fraction $L(R)$ of actual expenditure (which amounts to the equation $P_t y_t = [1 + L(R)_t]^{-1}[S_{t-1} - qWk_t]$). Realized incomes are then distributed, new expectations are formed, and the model enters year $t + 1$. That is easier said than done, of course. The precise way in which disappointed expectations are revised is perhaps the most important and least understood determinant of the short-run dynamics of such a model. I do not propose to make even vague remarks about that process now.

Instead I shall proceed in a different way. One can imagine a sort of medium-run equilibrium for such an economy,

whose defining characteristic is that expectations are vali-
dated. I call it a medium-run, rather than long-run, equilibrium because it may involve excess profits or unbearable
losses. To get to a long-run equilibrium would require
modeling a process of entry or exit – investment or disinvest-
ment – that would eventually eliminate excess profits or
losses. In addition, I would have to settle the questions about
labor-market equilibrium that I have deliberately left unre-
solved. That is not on my agenda. I want to stop at the
medium-run stage.

To that end, I must ask what this model looks like when
two things are done to it. First, all differences between
expected and realized prices and quantities are eliminated.
That is, expectational equilibrium rules. Second, all time
subscripts are obliterated. That is, nothing changes from one
year to the next. The model economy is then in what I have
called medium-run equilibrium. The short-run dynamics
have worked themselves out (assuming a certain kind of
stability) and the long-run dynamics have not yet come into
play. What can be said about medium-run equilibrium?

## Medium-run equilibrium

The first necessary step is to eliminate lags and expectational
errors, as just described. If there is enough labor to meet
demand, the model reduces to the following six equations,
easily obtained from what has already been said:

$$\alpha P k^{t\tau-1} f'(n) = w$$
$$k^\tau f(n) = y$$
$$[1 + L(R)]Py + Wqk = \bar{M}$$
$$Wqk = \sigma(g(n)/q)\bar{M}$$
$$Py = Wnk + RWqk$$
$$M = \frac{1-\sigma(R)}{1+\frac{1}{L(R)}}\bar{M}$$

The only new symbol is $\bar{M}$, which stands for the total money supply, a parameter: remember that $M$ is the stock of money willingly held by the household sector throughout each year. The difference is temporarily in the hands of firms, who will eventually pay it out in wages and dividends.

These equations can be interpreted directly. The first two, just as before, say that firms choose the surplus-maximizing price, and stay on their demand curves. The third equation explains the role of $\bar{M}$. For one instant in each year, households hold all the money. They have just received as income the sales proceeds of all firms. So $\bar{M}$ is what I have previously called $S$. The "fact" that the financial resources of households coincide with the money supply is just a consequence of the "fact" that firms do not hold any permanent cash balances, and the "fact" that capital goods turn over in one period. This peculiarity could easily be eliminated. The third equation reports that households divide their resources among consumption spending, planned cash balances, and purchases of equity in the amount needed to finance investment. The fourth equation clears the capital market. The fifth states that the sales proceeds of the consumer-goods sector are exhausted by the payment of wages and dividends (including depreciation). The last equation describes the household demand for money.

These equations can be thought of as determining six endogenous variables – $y$, $P$, $R$, $M$, $n$, and $k$ – in terms of two exogenous variables, $\bar{M}$ and $W$. (Since $nk$ is total employment, it is determined too.) This is clearly a complete macroeconomic model, though a highly aggregative one. But it is just as clearly "loosely abstracted" from a micro model. The microeconomic origins are visible, very close to the surface.

It is instructive that one can also see in this model a family relationship to ISLM. The capital-market-clearing equation serves much the same purpose as an IS curve, although it was developed according to its own, slightly different, logic.

Similarly, the demand-for-money equation, supplemented by the definition of aggregate household resources, plays the role of an LM curve. There seems to be no reason why this family resemblance should not survive the addition to the model of a fully specified labor market.

The model also has a natural homogeneity property. It is easy to see that any equal proportional change in $\bar{M}$ and $W$ will simply change $P$ and $M$ in the same proportion, leaving all the real characteristics $(n, k, y, R)$ exactly as they were. This observation suggests that one could isolate the real side of the model by replacing the price level as a variable by the real wage $(w = W/P)$ and replacing the exogenously given money supply and nominal wage by the money supply measured in wage units $(\bar{m} = \bar{M}/W)$. This is easily and obviously done. With a little more algebra, the real side of the model can be reduced to two equations in two unknowns, $n$ and $k$. Those equations are

$$k = q^{-1}\sigma(g(n)/q)\bar{m}$$

$$k = \frac{\bar{m}}{[1 + L(g(n)/q)][n + g(n)] + q}.$$

If these two equations can be solved for $n$ and $k$, it is straightforward to recover the remaining real unknowns. In the rest of this chapter, my job is to say what I can about the medium-run equilibria of this model, and then to recapitulate its lessons for macroeconomics with imperfectly competitive micro foundations.

The first equation says that $k$ is an increasing function of $n$. A higher labor–capital ratio in the consumption-goods sector implies a higher rate of return (according to equation (4)) and a higher return on equity implies a higher demand for equity. It is hard to be more specific; but it is certainly possible that the demand for equity increases only very gently when the expected net dividend rate is only slightly positive, then rises more sharply as the return on equity becomes more interesting, and might even taper off again as households find themselves saving a lot and putting it into equity. Thus the graph of this equation might have a sort of S-shape.

In the second equation, $L(R)$ is the demand for money. It certainly decreases as the dividend rate increases. It might even have a reverse S-shape: when the return on equity is fairly low, the demand for money decreases slowly, then more rapidly as equity becomes more attractive, but it must flatten out eventually as household cash balances per unit of consumer expenditure get near their practical minimum. The factor $n + g(n)$ is always increasing with $n$. So the graph of this equation could in principle have one or two turning points. I have drawn a configuration in which there are three intersections. This brief discussion does not constitute an argument, of course. I am merely exhibiting one among several possibilities.

The implication is that the model can have three medium-run equilibria for a given value of the money supply in wage units (figure 2.1). If we compare these equilibrium configurations with each other, it will always be the case that higher investment and higher employment go together. On the maintained assumption that there is enough labor to go around, more employment and output are preferred to less. So the three equilibria can be ranked: bigger is better. If this economy were in one of the lower-employment equilibria, it would be a good idea to move it to a higher one, if there were some way of doing that.

Here is a subtler point. The dividend rate is unambiguously higher in an equilibrium with higher investment, a higher labor–capital ratio, and therefore higher employment. If there were constant returns to scale in the consumption sector, it would follow that the equilibrium real wage would be lower as the return on equity got higher. But increasing returns to scale overturns that presumption. The real wage could rise or fall as the economy moves to equilibria with higher and higher employment and output.

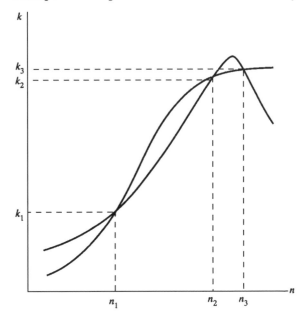

*Figure 2.1*

All of this is with a given real money supply. Corresponding to *each* of the equilibria just described, there is a whole family of equilibria traced out for different values of $\bar{m}$. These are of a special kind. It can be checked from the two equations that they can be written as equations in $n$ and $k/\bar{m}$. Thus when $\bar{m}$ changes, $k$ is simply proportional to $\bar{m}$, and $n$ does not change at all. The volume of investment and capital is proportional to the money supply in wage units, and the labor–capital ratio in the consumer-goods sector is independent of it. It follows that employment in the consumer-goods sector and, in fact, total employment, are also proportional to $\bar{m}$. (Total employment is $(n + q)k$.) No particular significance should be attached to this simple proportionality. It comes primarily from the convenient but inessential assumption that investment goods are produced by labor alone, under constant returns.

Now I want to look more closely at any one "family" of equilibria. The fact that there can easily be several such families is a consequence of the particular model I have been developing. But the existence of a one-parameter continuum of equilibria *within* each family is perfectly routine. It is exactly analogous to the intersections traced out along an IS curve by a shifting LM curve as the real money supply is varied parametrically, and it depends on my taking it for granted that the labor market allows an interval of possible equilibrium levels of employment. Nevertheless this particular model has some interesting things to say about the equilibria within any one family.

If the money supply is increased (or the nominal wage decreased) by $x$ percent, the output of consumption goods increases more than proportionally, i.e., by more than $x$ percent. Thus output per worker increases, and so does the real wage. Within any family, higher steady-state output and employment is accompanied by a *higher* real wage. Increasing returns to scale is the essential source of this result. If we are holding the nominal wage constant, the price of consumer goods must fall. If the money supply is held constant and the nominal wage is reduced exogenously, the price level must fall more than proportionally. The conclusion about real wages and employment is intrinsic to the model.

I will make only one more observation about this complicated configuration of medium-run equilibria, with several discrete families and a continuum of possible situations within each family. A desired level of employment – perhaps full employment, if that is not too old fashioned a concept – can be achieved in principle within any of the families. It is only necessary to choose the right money supply (in wage units). The right money supply will differ from family to family, but suppose we knew what it was and could achieve it. Which is best? Is it better to reach full employment with a low labor–capital ratio in the consumer-goods sector but a high stock of capital, or with a highly labor-intensive consumer-goods sector and a small rate of investment? Presumably the appropriate criterion of choice is the output of consumer goods per person employed in both sectors. It turns out that there is no easy answer to that question. An answer can always be calculated, but I do not see that any general rule can be laid down in advance.

## Conclusions

More can be done with this model. Hahn and I have made some further explorations; but they are hard work and this is not the time for me to tell you about them in detail. I will mention only two results, because they support one of the general claims I made in the first chapter. The short-run behavior of this model depends on entrepreneurial quantity expectations. Firms in the consumption sector must protect the position of their demand curves. This opens the way to two questions. First, can optimism about demand be self-justifying? If firms expect favorable demand conditions and make the decisions that are appropriate to those expectations, is it possible that they will bring about conditions as good as or better than they had anticipated? The answer to that question is: yes, they can, but not always. It is possible to elucidate the conditions that favor the "bootstraps" outcome, but they are quite complicated. The second question is this: are the short-run expectational dynamics stable? Starting with disappointed expectations, will the model converge to a medium-run equilibrium? That is not an easy question at all. The answer must depend on the way in which falsified expectations are revised. All I can tell you is that under static expectations – this period is expected to be like the previous period actually was – both stability and instability are possible, and again one can elucidate the conditions that favor one over the other.

But I would really prefer to think of this particular model

as a vehicle for reflections on a broader theme: the enrichment of macroeconomic theory that comes from embedding it in a more realistic micro context, especially the combination of increasing returns to scale and monopolistic competition. Here I want to emphasize two further conclusions. The more general one echoes the first chapter: this sort of model can easily generate multiple equilibria. Is that just a curiosity? No simple model-building exercise can tell us. But it is worth stating that the possibility arises "naturally" and robustly. It may be even more significant that the results correspond well to the intuitions of many generations of economists who thought that such things might happen but lacked the analytical software to give exact form to their intuitions. So I am not arguing for a paradox, but a commonplace.

The multiplicity of equilibria has a further consequence. They cannot each be the best of all possible worlds. Dr. Pangloss might be at home in a world of constant returns to scale and perfect competition. In this other world he is necessarily an imperfect guide.

This is a good place for me to mention the second conclusion, a more specific one this time. The example I have presented to you shows that real wage rates may be *positively* correlated with employment across equilibria. This is both good news and bad news. The good news is that sometimes it may not be necessary to sacrifice real wages to achieve high employment. Increasing returns to scale, when they hold, work in the other direction. The bad news is that it must be harder to imagine a self-correcting labor market. Excessive unemployment would be expected to depress real (or at least nominal) wages, if it has any effect at all. If the goal is to move the economy to a new equilibrium with higher employment, this is a step in the wrong direction. One can imagine ways around this obstacle but that is not something that, as Americans say, you can take to the bank.

In any case, we are now pretty far from the anthropomorphic picture of the macroeconomy as acting out the lifetime optimizing plan of a single self-contained consumer-cum-producer. That is perhaps a goal to be achieved, surely not an assumption to be made.

## Bibliographical note

Anyone interested in the model of this chapter should look at F. H. Hahn and R. M. Solow, *A Critical Essay on Macroeconomic Theory*, MIT Press, 1995. Chapter 4 develops the microfoundations for this model in much greater detail; and chapter 6 analyzes more aspects of the macro model than one lecture can do. In particular, chapter 6 is not limited to the medium-run equilibrium. It deals also with short-run dynamics, when the firm's expectations about next period's aggregate output and consumer-goods price level are formed adaptively. The appendix to chapter 6 then exhibits a few computer simulations of the short-run dynamic model. When the configuration is as shown in figure 2.1 of this chapter, the two outer equilibria are stable, in the sense that some initial conditions lead to one of them, and nearly all other initial conditions start trajectories that go to the other outer equilibrium. The middle medium-run equilibrium is unstable. When the configuration is changed, so that the relative slopes of the two curves are reversed at intersections, the middle equilibrium becomes the stable one, and the two outer equilibria appear to be unstable.

There are many ways to construct an aggregative model on imperfectly competitive foundations. A near neighbor in the literature is Y.-K. Ng, "A Micro-Macroeconomic Analysis Based on a Representative Firm," *Economica* 49 (1982) 121–39.

A practical problem with a model like the one in this chapter is that it is not at all clear how to calibrate it. Our folk-intuition for the values of macroeconomic parameters comes from a vast volume of empirical work, most of it within the framework of a roughly Keynesian model. (The

"Real Business Cycle" school is now engaged in developing its own folklore in the same way.) That does not help much in dealing with a model that uses rather different categories.

The observation that labor productivity tends to be procyclical goes back to Fabricant, *Employment in Manufacturing, 1899–1939: An Analysis of Its Relation to the Volume of Production*, NBER 1942, and was developed further by Brechling ("The Relationship between Output and Employment in British Manufacturing Industries," *Review of Economic Studies*, July 1965) and others. A good survey of the state of play at that time can be found in N. J. Ireland and D. J. Smyth, "The Specification of Short-Run Employment Models," *Review of Economic Studies*, April 1970, 281–5.

This observation leads naturally to the question whether there are short-run increasing returns to labor, because the stock of capital is nearly constant on the business-cycle time scale. This interpretation would contravene the formulation used here. But it has recently been challenged by C. Burnside, M. Eichenbaum, and S. Rebelo, "Capital Utilization and Returns to Scale," NBER Working Paper No. 5125, May 1995. They opt for constant returns to scale, but in fact their argument bears mostly on returns to labor.

They make a good case that short-run increasing returns to labor is an illusion. It is a fact that labor input increases less than proportionately with output in business-cycle upswings. If capital input were indeed more or less constant, one would naturally infer increasing returns to labor. But we know only that the stock of capital can change very little in a short interval. But capital *input*, the services drawn from the stock per unit time, may also be rising, either because machinery is turned on for more hours per week, or because some machinery that had been turned off is turned on. If, for example, capital input were rising at the same rate as labor input (so that capital intensity remains constant), the natural inference would be increasing returns to *scale*, not to labor. If the flow of the services of capital were actually more variable over the business cycle than the flow of labor input, then the cyclical pattern could be compatible with constant returns to scale and diminishing returns to each factor. The trouble is that the flow of capital services is hard to measure.

Burnside, Eichenbaum, and Rebelo try various devices, including the use of purchased electricity by industry as a measure of the intensity of use of capital. Their preferred conclusion is constant returns to scale, but that does not appear to be a very robust inference. (If the world were like the model of this chapter, I would expect the parameter $\tau$ that measures increasing returns to scale to be roughly 1.10 or 1.15 which would be empirically barely distinguishable from 1.00.) Many years ago I played around with similar ideas ("Some Evidence on the Short-Run Productivity Puzzle," in *Development and Planning: Essays in Honor of Paul Rosenstein Rodan*, Allen and Unwin, 1972, pages 316–25), including the use of electricity as a proxy for capital input, and came to similar, though not identical, conclusions.

Something more basic may be going on here, however. The model in the text adopts the common presupposition that the firm actually uses all the capital in place. We all know, however, that firms often have unused capacity. That is, they leave some capital idle. In the particular model used in this lecture, the output and employment decisions are made irrevocably at the same time as the investment decision. If that were literally the case, then there would be no occasion for unused capacity. It is not literally the case, however; a better model might allow an option for late revision of production plans. Then a firm wishing to cut back would need some way of allocating the cutback between idle capital and lower employment. It is even more important, of course, that most productive capital is durable, so that firms can and do respond to falling demand by leaving some of their capacity idle, all week long, as with labor.

# Part II

# 3

## Monopolistic competition and the multiplier

### 1 Motivation

The trained instinct of the modern rigorous economist is to reach first for the Walrasian model. Maybe it is – like the Army, Navy, Air Force, and Marines – a great place to start. Most of us, however, live with the ineradicable feeling that large and important areas of economic life cannot be described in that way. One of the admirable things about Kenneth Arrow's work is that even while making major contributions to the perfection of the Walrasian model, he has never blinked its deficiencies and has sought for alternatives more suited to the facts of life in modern industrial economies.

What follows is a very preliminary step in that direction. This particular story leaves very large gaps of its own. I will leave until the end my own appreciation of what they are. Some of them are patched up in a more complete and therefore more complicated version of the model that will appear as my 1985 Mitsui Lectures at the University of Birmingham.

My immediate starting point is the article by Martin

I thank John Moore and Martin Weitzman for helpful comments.
Reprinted from
*Equilibrium Analysis*
*Essays in Honor of Kenneth J. Arrow, Volume II*
Edited by Walter P. Heller, Ross M. Starr, and David A. Starrett

Weitzman (1982). My goal is to marry it to the simplest model of effective demand. In his article, Weitzman argued that the natural habitat of any theory of persistent involuntary unemployment is an economy with nontrivial increasing returns to scale. The main reason he gives is that otherwise it is impossible to explain why bits of unemployed resources do not form tiny scale replicas of the going economy and thus employ themselves. Each such minieconomy would be at least as productive as the full economy and able to support itself on its own self-generated demand.

It is not even necessary to go so far as the minieconomy. Minifirms, once formed from previously unemployed resources, could sell their minioutput on competitive markets. Balanced expansion takes care of the rest. If only labor is unemployed, "nonincreasing returns to scale in lending" would permit an atom of labor to borrow the purchasing power needed to hire cooperating inputs, and any infinitesimal bidding up of factor prices could be covered by the preexisting gap between the wage and the marginal disutility of labor.

To put the point slightly differently, any theory of persistent involuntary unemployment must account for the economy's inability to organize the Pareto-improving transactions that must be available. If those transactions could take place in a backyard, or on the head of a pin, it is hard to see what might prevent them. But if there is a substantial minimum scale for viable economic activity, there is at least the possibility of a plausible account of coordination failure, though of course it remains the job of theory to give that account.

This line of argument is quite general. Weitzman's formalization is of the following kind. Imagine any kind of general equilibrium model and suppose it possesses a solution, that is, an ordinary full-employment equilibrium, when the supply of labor $L$ is inelastic. For expositional convenience, we can imagine the equilibrium solution to be unique, though that is not at all essential. Ordinarily, if there is an equilibrium with labor supply $L_0$, there will be an equilibrium for a range of smaller labor supplies $L_0$. Now nothing prevents us from thinking of the equilibrium with employment $L = (1 - u)L_0$ as an equilibrium with unemployment rate $u$ *provided* we have a good story explaining how the economy can be at rest with a volume of unemployment $uL_0$. The role of increasing returns to scale is to permit the telling of such a story.

In a model with increasing returns to scale, one of the essential characteristics of an equilibrium is the *number* of firms. In comparing two equilibria – in the sense just described – it will often be found that the equilibrium with the higher level of employment has both a larger number of firms and larger output per firm. But then, for instance, if the equilibrium concept requires zero profits, the equilibrium with higher employment will also have the higher (real) wage. The makings of an unemployment equilibrium story are clearly there. Real wage cutting in the presence of unemployment would be a step in the wrong direction. Price cutting in the hope of exploiting increasing returns by enlarging the market would be a step in the right direction; but since profits are initially zero, price cutting would involve immediate certain losses in the hope of future profits, which might not materialize anyway given that the new equilibrium will also be characterized by zero profits. That is hardly a theory, but it is certainly the promise of a theory.

I owe to James Meade the somewhat different point that nominal wage reduction might be the right reaction to unemployment provided that economic policy maintains aggregate nominal expenditure and firms respond by the even greater price reductions that are permitted by de-creasing costs.

A model featuring nontrivial increasing returns to scale cannot have perfect competition as its market structure. The particular model used by Weitzman as a vehicle for his reasoning is a version of the Hotelling–Lancaster–Salop model of monopolistic competition with a circular product space, and the equilibrium concept is symmetric Chamberlinian. In the next section, I describe a modified version of Weitzman's model. The modifications are of two kinds. The first is merely technical, to correct a minor implausibility in the original formulation. The second is more substantial: I modify the demand side by introducing autonomous expenditures, in preparation for analyzing the short- and long-run response of the model to shifts in aggregate demand. The presence of an exogenous source of demand has the effect of tying down the level of employment.

## 2  A model

There is fundamentally only one produced good, but it can come in a continuum of "qualities," represented by points on the circumference of a circle of length $H$. Households are uniformly distributed around the circle with unit density. To say that a household is "located" at a particular point on the circle means that it prefers the quality represented by that point. A household consuming $x$ units of the good at distance $h$ from its own location achieves a utility level $u(x, h)$, where $u$ is increasing and concave in $x$ but decreasing and (probably) convex in $h$. Weitzman set $u = x - ah$, but that seems inappropriate because it makes the loss of utility with distance independent of the quantity consumed and the marginal utility of consumption independent of quality. Instead, I shall work with the utility function $xu(h)$ with $u' < 0$ and, where it matters, $u'' > 0$. Linearity in $x$ serves a useful purpose: Each household will consume only one quality (or, at worst, be indifferent between a neighboring pair). Besides, it aggregates well. Obvious examples are $xe^{-ah}$ and $xh^{-a}$; I will refer to them later.

Eventually we will come down to a symmetric equilibrium

with $m$ firms equally spaced around the circle, thus at a distance $D = H/m$ from each other, and all charging the same price. That situation must be a Nash equilibrium in prices. So imagine a typical firm looking for its best price $p'$ when all other firms charge price $p$. The firm's market area will extend a distance $h$ on each side and thus be of length $2h$, where $h$ is determined by the condition that the consumer at that location be indifferent between the products of the two nearest firms, one at distance $h$ and the other at distance $D - h$. Consider the consumer spending $M$ units of "money" on the good. Indifference implies

$$\frac{M}{p'}u(h) = \frac{M}{p}u(D - h),$$

from which follows

$$\frac{p}{p'} = \frac{u(D - h)}{u(h)}.$$

Thus $h$ is unambiguously decreasing in $p'$ for given $p$. Later we will need the derivative

$$\frac{dh}{dp'} = \frac{p}{(p')^2}\frac{u(h)^2}{u(h)u'(D - h) + u(D - h)u'(h)}.$$

How much demand is generated from a market area of length $2h$ when the firm charges $p'$ and others charge $p$? Let aggregate employment in the whole economy be $L$, uniformly distributed around the circumference with density $L/H$. Let the wage, in unit of account, be $w$. Weitzman assumes that households spend all their earnings on the good, and there is no other source of demand. Here is my main deviation from his assumptions. Households spend a fixed fraction $c$ of their earnings on the good (or their price elasticity of demand is 1). Demand from this source is thus $(2h/H)(cwL/p')$.

In addition, there is (must be) another source of demand, government purchases, say, or perhaps, when the model can be extended that far, investment spending by firms. Suppose that nominal exogenous spending in unit of account is given; call it $G$. The goods bought are used in some way that does not affect private demand. I shall assume that this nominal demand is always equally allocated among firms, so each can count on $G/m$. Real demand from this source is thus $G/mp'$ for the typical firm. Notice first that firms are unable to discriminate against the government but must sell to all buyers at the same price. There is a second tacit assumption. It could have been assumed that exogenous spending is equally allocated over units of circumference rather than over firms. That would have been somewhat simpler, in fact; all demand would then have the same price elasticity, larger than unity because of the responsiveness of market area to own price. When exogenous spending is divided among firms, each firm's demand is the sum of household demand, with greater than unit elasticity, and its share of the unit-elastic exogenous demand. I think the extra complication is worth bearing precisely to allow the price elasticity of demand to vary with $c$ as well as with $m$, though I would not seriously defend this particular way of doing so.

The typical firm thus faces the demand function

$$d(p') = \frac{G}{mp'} + \frac{2h}{H}\frac{cwL}{p'}$$

and the revenue function

$$R(p') = p'D(p') = \frac{G}{m} + \frac{2h}{H}cwL.$$

Here, of course, $L$ and $m$ as well as $p$ are parameters to the firm.

On the production side, I follow Weitzman exactly. Let $y$ and $n$ be output and employment of the typical firm. Then

$$y = k(n - f),$$

where the positive constant $f$ stands for the setup labor that is the source of increasing returns. Output is zero unless $n$ exceeds $f$. It follows that the total, average, and marginal costs associated with output $y$ are

$$\text{TC} = w\left(\frac{y}{k} + f\right), \ \text{AC} = w\left(\frac{1}{k} + \frac{f}{y}\right), \ \text{MC} = \frac{w}{k}.$$

As in any Chamberlinian large group, the firm maximizes profits by charging a price at which

$$\text{MR} = \frac{dR}{dy} = \frac{R'(p')}{d'(p')} = \text{MC} = \frac{w}{k}.$$

The detailed calculations make use of the formula for $dh/dp'$ set down earlier. Furthermore, for a symmetric equilibrium, we can set $p' = p$ and $2h = H/m$ after differentiation. The final result is

$$p = \frac{w}{k}\left[1 + 2\left(-\frac{H}{2m}\frac{u'(H/2m)}{u(H/2m)}\right)\left(1 + \frac{G}{Z}\right)\right], \tag{1}$$

where, for temporary ease of notation, $Z = cwL$, which is aggregate nominal spending out of wage income. In addition, we can always write

$$mpy = G + Z, \tag{2}$$

and in symmetric equilibrium,

$$y = k\left(\frac{L}{m} - f\right). \tag{3}$$

As a final condition for long-run Chamberlinian equilibrium, suppose that free entry determines the number of firms, $m$, so that

$$p = \text{AC} = w\left(\frac{1}{k} + \frac{f}{y}\right). \tag{4}$$

It can be checked immediately that equations (3) and (4) are equivalent to (3) and

$$mpy = wL. \tag{5}$$

Now (2) and (5) can be combined to rewrite (1) as

$$p = \frac{w}{k}\left[1 + \frac{2}{c}\left(-\frac{H}{2m}\frac{u'(H/2m)}{u(H/2m)}\right)\right]. \tag{1'}$$

Here the long-run equilibrium price is represented as a markup on marginal cost. One can easily check that the markup factor is exactly what it should be, expressible in terms of the elasticity of demand faced by each firm in a long-run equilibrium or in terms of Lerner's *degree of monopoly*. The markup factor is larger if the (absolute) elasticity of $u(\cdot)$ is larger at equilibrium and if the propensity to spend wage income is smaller. A very elastic $u(\cdot)$ means that different qualities of the good are relatively poor substitutes for one another; this gives each firm more monopoly power in the obvious way. The role of $c$ is also simple. It will be remembered that each firm's demand curve is the sum of two components: autonomous demand with unit elasticity and household demand with greater than unit elasticity. The combined elasticity therefore exceeds 1 and is larger when $c$ is larger so that the component with a bigger demand elasticity gets heavier weight.

## 3 Variations

Here I digress for a moment. It is plain that this is a Chamberlinian large-group equilibrium only by courtesy. Each firm has two neighbors whose reaction to its own decisions it cannot ignore. If one really believed in this world, it would need to be analyzed as a chain of linked oligopolies. It would be easy to hint vaguely that "quality" could be many-dimensional, so that a firm might have many immediate neighbors. Then the effects of its own price decisions would be diffused over all of them and ignored by each of them as the model requires.

In two recent papers (1985a and b), Oliver Hart has shown just how complicated it can be actually to carry out this program. Nevertheless, I think it is fair to take his results as offering a license to proceed as if we were dealing with a true large group. With enough work, it could be fixed up.

In his analysis, Hart takes it to be a desideratum that the elasticity of demand facing a typical firm should *not* go to infinity as the number of firms increases without limit. That requirement makes sense if one's goal is to prove the existence of a true Chamberlinian equilibrium of monopolistic competition. For my purpose, however, it is just as interesting to contemplate cases in which the perfectly competitive limit *is* reached as the number of firms gets large. I want to point out, therefore, that equation (1') can exhibit either kind of behavior, depending on the particular choice of the substitution function $u(h)$.

From (1'), the limiting situation is perfectly competitive if $-hu'(h)/u(h)$ goes to zero with $h$. The limiting situation (with large $m$) is monopolistically competitive if $-hu'(h)/u(h)$ goes to a nonzero limit as $h$ goes to zero. Here are some examples:

a. Suppose $u(h) = e^{-ah}$. Then $-hu'(h)/u(h) = ah$ and (1') becomes

$$p = \frac{w}{k}\left[1 + \frac{aH}{mc}\right].$$

Here price goes to marginal cost as the number of firms gets large in equilibrium.

b. If $u(h) = h^{-a}$, of course, $-hu'(h)/u(h) = a$. Then

$$p = \frac{w}{k}\left(1 + \frac{2a}{c}\right),$$

and the markup is independent of the number of firms. This is an interesting borderline case and I shall comment on it later.

c. Suppose we would like to have

$$-hu'(h)/u(h) = s + th$$

for positive constants $s$ and $t$. Then the markup will decrease to $s$ as the number of firms become infinite (and increase to infinity as the number of firms tends to "zero"). The differential equation is easily integrated to give

$$u(h) = h^{-s}e^{-th}.$$

The fact that here and in example (b) $u$ is unbounded as $h$ goes to zero is unimportant, because almost no household gets to consume its very favorite quality.

d. If $-hu'(h)/u(h) = (Ah + B)/(h + C)$, then the markup goes to a nonzero value $B/C$ as $m$ becomes infinite and to a finite value as $m$ tends to zero. To make sense, we need to choose $A$ bigger than $B/C$. Once again, the differential equation can be integrated to yield

$$u(h) = h^{-B/C}(h + C)^{-(A-B/C)},$$

which has all the necessary properties.

e. Finally, one might wonder if it is possible that the equilibrium markup might rise with $m$. (Perverse as that sounds, we have already found a case in which the markup is independent of $m$.) For that to happen, it must be that $(d/dh)(-hu'(h)/u(h)) < 0$. But $(d/dh)(-hu'(h)/u(h))$ has the sign of $h(u')^2 - uu' - hu''$, so this alternative pattern is possible if $u''$ is positive and sufficiently large. In that case, the equilibrium real wage falls as aggregate output increases. Higher output is accomplished by a more than proportional increase in the number of firms and a reduction in output per firm. Output per worker falls, and so does the real wage. In the borderline constant-elasticity case (b) above, output per firm is constant and changes in equilibrium output occur entirely through changes in the number of firms. A sharply convex $u(\cdot)$ contributes to this outcome because the marginal demand for greater variety intensifies as variety increases. Thus the degree of monopoly is greater even with a larger number of firms. This is presumably an unlikely case.

It should be remembered that the equilibrium number of

firms is endogenous in this model. I have spoken of "varying" the number of firms just for clarity. But $f$, the level of fixed costs, is a parameter; and clearly the equilibrium value of $m$ goes to zero as $f$ goes to infinity and to infinity as $f$ goes to zero. So there is no harm done.

## 4  The case without autonomous spending

From here on, I adopt the parameterization $u(h) = e^{-ah}$ so that I can give concrete results. It seems to be the most reasonable simple formula.

To establish the analogy to Weitzman's model, I first set $G = 0$ and $c = 1$. Then equation (2) collapses to equation (5), and there are only three independent equations, (1), (3), and (5), in the unknowns $p$, $y$, $m$, and $L$. The model economy can be in long-run Chamberlinian equilibrium with any level of employment. Then equation (1) reads

$$p = \frac{w}{k}\left(1 + \frac{aH}{m}\right),$$

and a complete solution of the model gives

$$m = \frac{aH}{2}\left[-1 + \left(1 + \frac{4L}{aHf}\right)^{1/2}\right],$$

$$p = \frac{w}{k}\left[1 + \frac{2}{-1 + [1 + (4L/aHf)]^{1/2}}\right],$$

$$y = \frac{2kL/aH}{1 + [1 + (4L/aHf)]^{1/2}}.$$

Note that $m$ does indeed go from infinity to zero as $f$ goes from zero to infinity. Note also that higher employment carries with it an increase in the number of firms, in output per firm, *and* in the real wage. [In the case $u(h) = h^{-a}$, the equilibrium number of firms is proportional to $L$, and output per firm and the real wage are independent of $L$.]

If this economy were to find itself in a zero-profit Chamberlinian equilibrium with unemployment, "all" it needs to set things right is for just enough new firms to appear. The added demand generated by the workers they hire will permit all firms to expand. Decreasing cost will allow the price to fall. As Weitzman pointed out, the only noncooperative way for new firms to come into existence would be to wedge themselves "between" already existing firms and force a realignment of market areas. Since the existing firms have zero profits and entering firms might have to start small, the prospect is for all-round losses, perhaps never to be made up. Of course, there may be dynamic paths starting with "nominal" wage reductions that lead to full equilibrium at higher employment. It is hard to say, if only because there is no true monetary side to the model. But it is far from obvious that a decentralized economy could find such a path quickly, even if there is one.

The fact that this model can be in neutral equilibrium at any level of employment is a consequence of the assumption, a sort of Say's law, that directs all wage income – the only income there is in equilibrium – into consumption. As soon as that assumption is dropped, the situation changes.

## 5  Autonomous spending: long run

When $G$ is positive and $c < 1$, the degree of freedom disappears. Exogenous expenditure fixes the scale of the economy. The mathematical counterpart is that equations (1)–(4) now define a unique equilibrium in $p$, $y$, $m$, and $L$. Perhaps it should be mentioned explicitly that I treat the nominal wage $w$ as given. This is not an assumption of "rigid wages" but merely a choice of *numéraire*. (I am, of course, assuming throughout that the real wage does not clear the labor market.) There is nothing in the model to determine the price level in terms of unit of account. Now it should be understood that exogenous spending is really given in wage units, not in nominal terms.

Remembering that $Z = cwL$, one sees right away that equations (2) and (5) imply that $mpy = G/(1 - c)$. Across zero-profit equilibria, the simplest of all multiplier formulas holds, and for the usual reason.

In this model, however, aggregate income is the product of three endogenous variables: output per firm, the price of the good (in wage units), and the number of firms. The model can be solved for each of these, with the results

$$p = \frac{w}{k}\left[1 + \frac{2}{-1 + \left(1 + \frac{4cG/w}{(1-c)faH}\right)^{1/2}}\right]$$

$$L = \frac{G/w}{1 - c},$$

$$m = \frac{aH}{2c}\left[-1 + \left(1 + \frac{4cG/w}{(1-c)faH}\right)^{1/2}\right],$$

$$y = k\left(\frac{L}{m} - f\right).$$

These bear a family resemblance to the corresponding formulas for the closed model with no autonomous demand. The ratio of price to marginal cost is higher the bigger is $a$. This is because large $a$ confers more monopoly power on the firm by making alternative qualities less good substitutes. The parameter $c$ enters in two ways. A small $c$ weights the firm's demand in favor of the less elastic autonomous expenditure but also reduces aggregate demand. The net effect is to reduce output per firm and raise price; the effect on the number of firms is more complicated.

This particular parameterization of the model retains the convenient feature that changes in $G$, and thus in aggregate economic activity, work themselves out by changing employment, the number of firms, and output per firm in the same direction. The real wage moves *with* employment. I describe this as an advantage not because of any claim to descriptive realism but rather because it puts the key question of the dynamics of adjustment into sharp relief. To get further with that question, however, I define a short run for this model in the next section.

## 6 Autonomous spending: the short-run multiplier

The comparative-static adjustments explicit and implicit in the preceding section are strictly long run in character. The response to a change in $G$ is a movement from one free-entry zero-profit Chamberlinian equilibrium to another; and it is achieved in this case by entry or exit of firms, if it can be achieved at all. It is more natural to think of the model's short-run response to changes in $G$ as the profit-maximizing reactions of the existing firms, along with the associated profits, positive or negative. After all, these are the signals that are supposed to induce the appropriate long-run adjustments. Nothing much is lost and some simplicity is gained, however, if short-run responses are assumed to start from a position of long-run equilibrium.

Thus, in the short run, equation (4) is dropped and $m$ is treated as a constant [but a constant that satisfies equations (4) and (5) initially]. The short-run comparative statics of $p$, $y$, and $L$ come from equations (1)–(3). Actually, it is enough to work with just $p$ and $y$, taking account of the fact that (3) and the definition of $Z$ define $Z$ as a function of $y$ alone, with $dZ/dy = cwm/k$. The variational equations are

$$\left( \begin{array}{cc} \dfrac{1}{y} & \dfrac{aHG/c(kL)^2}{p - cw/k} \end{array} \right) \left( \begin{array}{c} dp/dG \\ dy/dG \end{array} \right) = \left( \begin{array}{c} aH/mckL \\ 1/m \end{array} \right). \tag{6}$$

From (6), after a lot of maneuvers making heavy use of the fact that the state variables satisfy (1), (2), and (5), one can calculate the multiplier formula

$$\frac{d(mpy)}{dG} = \frac{1}{(1 - c)(1 + q + q^2)^{-1}}. \tag{7}$$

Here $q = aH/mc$. In this version of the short-run model, equation (1) reads

$$p = \frac{w}{k}\left[1 + \frac{aH}{m}\left(1 + \frac{G}{cwL}\right)\right].$$

Evaluated at the initial long-run zero-profit equilibrium, the last parenthesis is just $1/c$. Hence $q$ is the markup. The short-run multiplier is larger when the elasticity of demand is larger, that is, the degree of monopoly is smaller. If $q$ is near zero (the elasticity of demand is near infinite), the multiplier approaches the long-run value of $(1 - c)^{-1}$. As $q$ approaches infinity (the elasticity of demand approaches unity, its smallest permissible value), the multiplier goes to 1.

The reason for this is not mysterious. In the short run, rise in $G$ – an upward shift in demand – permits positive profits to emerge before they are competed away by entry. In the model, these profits are not spent, and that limits the size of the multiplier. One could introduce a positive marginal propensity to spend profits with more or less obvious consequences. [If the same marginal propensity to spend applies to all income, then (2) says $mpy = G + cmpy$, and there is nothing more to be said.] But I have something ultimately more ambitious in mind. I have referred to production units as firms, but they are really just units of capacity devoted to profit maximization. Wherever I have said *entry* I could have said *investment*. One way to study the all-important dynamics of transition from short run to long run under increasing returns to scale would be to try to incorporate a serious theory of investment. According to what was said earlier, this may be the key to the notion of unemployment equilibrium. Anything so mechanical as a marginal propensity to invest profits would miss all the deeper questions about the ability of the unmanaged economy to organize the Pareto improvements that spell the difference between prosperity and recession.

In the short run, both $p$ and $y$ change in the same direction as $G$. Since the nominal wage is a parameter, the real wage falls when employment rises and vice versa. This is not what actually happens in the real world, but it is nevertheless a useful reminder that short-run forces may be perverse with respect to the achievement of long-run goals. It happens this way in the model because firms operate freely in a spot market for labor; the model concentrates on other things.

It is possible to work out the proportions in which a change in $py$ is divided between change in $y$ and change in $p$ (or $p/w$). As it happens, the ratio of the percentage change in $p$ to the percentage change in $y$, when $G$ varies, is $q^2/(1 + q)$. Alternatively, one can decompose $d(py)dG$ into $p\, dy/dG$ and $y\, dp/dG$ with the result that

$$\frac{p\,dy}{dG} = \frac{1+q}{1+q+q^2}\frac{d(py)}{dG}\,, \qquad \frac{y\,dp}{dG} = \frac{q^2}{1+q+q^2}\frac{d(py)}{dG}\,.$$

These are intuitive: A high elasticity of demand makes for a relatively small change in price and a relatively large change in output.

To fix orders of magnitude, an elasticity of demand equal to three means $q = \frac{1}{2}$. Then six-sevenths of the multiplier change in nominal output is real, and the remaining one-seventh is the change in price in wage units or, with opposite sign, the change in the real wage. The demand elasticity must get down to about 1.6–1.7 for the division between price and output change to be 50:50. The effects on the numerical value of the multiplier are more dramatic. Suppose $c = \frac{1}{2}$, so the ordinary Keynesian multiplier is 2. Then $q = \frac{1}{2}$ reduces the short-run multiplier to 1.4, and $q = 1.6$ reduces it to 1.1.

It is the essence of this formulation that short-run movements above and below long-term equilibrium are accompanied by positive or negative profits. Ultimately, it will be the investment induced by those profits that drives longer-run changes – and probably magnifies short-run fluctuations in the process. I have followed that trail for a bit in my Mitsui

Lectures. For now, I just record the relevant comparative-statics derivative. If we set aggregate profit $P = mpy - wL$, then it is easily reckoned that

$$\frac{dp}{dG} = \frac{q(1+q)}{1+q+q^2} \cdot M,$$

where $M$ is the multiplier evaluated in (7) above. Thus, if $q = \frac{1}{2}$ (the elasticity of demand is 3), profits amount to three-sevenths of the increment in income, whereas if $q = 1.6$, profits absorb 80 percent of the short-run change in income. This formula provides the weights one would use to introduce a simple marginal propensity to spend profits. But I have already argued for a different way to proceed.

## 7  Conclusions

It is not especially the function of simple models like this to provide prototypes for larger descriptive models. I think their purpose is rather to give "pure" illustrations of general principles. What principles emerge here?

First, further development of the model offers some confirmation of Weitzman's insight that the unassisted price mechanism may find it hard to extract an imperfectly competitive increasing returns-to-scale economy from an underemployment trap. Small-scale myopic adjustments could be self-frustrating. There are too many local Nash equilibria. Noncooperative outcomes may be inferior to what can be achieved by cooperative organization.

Second, the model suggests that the difference in orientation between investment and consumption may be fundamental, just as we used to think before Walrasian concepts and Walrasian notation infiltrated macroeconomic theory. The desirability of "pump priming" – getting a process started that will later, but only later, be self-sustaining – hinges on both the lumpiness and the durability of additions to capacity. Obviously expectations matter, including expectations about the behavior of other players, and thus another role for cooperative solutions opens up. The microeconomic foundations of macroeconomics might find room for strategic theories of investment.

Third, it may be a waste of time to try to construct macroeconomics on perfectly competitive foundations. That is already implied by increasing returns. But the model goes further in strongly suggesting that the behavior characteristics of the system, especially in the short run, may be sensitive to details of market structure.

## 8  Apologies

I have left to the very end my apology for the crudities of this deliberate reversion to simple 45-degree-line textbook Keynesianism. The point was to see if that old dog could produce some new tricks when placed in an unconventional framework. It seems to me that it has done so. But the crudities remain. The main ones are the treatment – or lack of treatment – of the asset market and the labor market.

With respect to the asset market, households save, but nothing is said about why they save or what they do with their savings. The most straightforward story is that households accumulate stocks of purchasing power in the form of "money." In turn, the government injects "new money" when it makes nominal expenditures. That will hardly do as anything more than a stopgap, if only because the motivation for saving is so nebulous. The key, obviously, is to introduce capital goods as a factor of production and, indirectly, a store of value. If investment is the mechanism by which the model economy gets from one long-run Nash equilibrium to another, then the financing of investment is fundamental to the outcome. The model needs some financial institutions so that household savings can finance the profit-motivated capital investments of firms. It is pretty clear how to proceed. The true difficulties with investment will come from the intrinsic uncertainty combined with economies of scale, not from the bare outlines.

With respect to the labor market, the model operates as if there is in the background an inelastically supplied labor force. Actual employment may be less than that, governed not by supply but by the price and output decisions of forms. The nominal wage is conventionally given, and the real wage is passively determined by the price of goods. If this situation is to be described as an "equilibrium," the relevant equilibrium concept must be something other than wage-mediated clearing of the labor market. I have not tried to specify an alternative concept according to which the labor market could be at rest with involuntary unemployment, except to suggest yet another reason why the Walrasian concept has little to recommend it: because the natural disequilibrium dynamics would be misdirected. After all these years that is hardly a satisfactory treatment of the labor market. Some action should emanate from the supply side as well, and a model of endogenous wage determination should be added. But even after all these years it is not completely clear what a good model of the labor market would be.

### References

Hart, O. (1985a), "Monopolistic competition in the spirit of Chamberlin: A general model," *Review of Economic Studies*, 52 (4): 529–46.

Hart, O. (1985b), "Monopolistic competition in the spirit of Chamberlin: Special results," *Economic Journal*, 95: 889–908.

Weitzman, M. (1982), "Increasing returns and the foundations of unemployment theory," *Economic Journal*, 92: 787–804.

# Index

# DATE DUE

| | | | |
|---|---|---|---|
| | | | |
| | | | |
| | | | |
| | | | |
| | | | |
| | | | |
| | | | |
| | | | |
| | | | |
| | | | |
| | | | |
| | | | |
| | | | |
| | | | |
| | | | |
| | | | |
| | | | |
| | | | |
| GAYLORD | | | PRINTED IN U.S.A. |